Stop Fighting About Money

# STOP
# FIGHTING
# ABOUT
# MONEY

## and start making it work for you

by Kaycee W. Krysty, CPA, CFP
and Kristianne Blake, CPA, CFP

BOSTON
·B·
BOOKS

*First Printing*

---

Library of Congress Cataloging in Publication Data

Kayceee W. Krysty, CPA, CFP
Kristianne Blake, CPA, CFP
    Stop Fighting About Money
    and Start Making it Work for You
    1. Finance, personal   I. Title

LC Card #: 89-061621

ISBN: 0-9616683-9-3

*To Michael and John —*
*for putting up with*
*our late nights,*
*long telephone conversations,*
*and evenings out-of-town*
*while we collaborated*
*on this book.*

# Table of Contents

# Preface

Ten years ago we each turned to our respective spouses and asked "How can two such smart people have no money?" Here we were, financial professionals ourselves, married to men with business educations, all gainfully employed. But we were not achieving the financial successes we had dreamed of in our newlywed days. What was going on?

For both personal and professional reasons we explored how couples can successfully manage their personal finances. We read everything we could get our hands on. We experimented ,repeatedly, on ourselves with a wide variety of techniques. And we put together a solid program that works for us and has worked for our clients. And you can make it work for you.

Our program focuses on the most difficult part of achieving financial success — *taking action*. It is relatively simple to figure out what you need to do: save money and get out of debt. But if you don't actually take any actions you will not succeed. Our program includes a variety of techniques designed to help you take action.

This book will provide you with specific, tested techniques to make financial success happen for you. These techniques get you talking about money together in a constructive way and move you forward to making the joint decisions that will determine your financial future. If one or both of you are short on the self-discipline it takes to make financial dreams a reality, these techniques will be invaluable. While there is ultimately no replacement for your own ability to say no to yourself or your spouse, our techniques will make it a lot easier.

We do not want to mislead you. Getting control of your financial life is not easy. Clearly, it requires time and energy. More importantly, it requires a strong desire to take charge of your financial life — to get it under control once and for all and to keep it there.

## WORKING TOGETHER

This is not a task you pass on to your partner and say, "Here dear, you do this." It requires a joint effort. Both of you must be actively involved to make your money work for you, not against you. This book will get you planning as partners. Throughout the book you will learn new ideas, perform exercises, and have discussions that will help you move forward as a team on your financial life together.

This teamwork will yield great rewards for you both. Decisions about spending will be made more consistently. You will know where you are financially. You will talk about money often and comfortably. You will be able to start a regular savings program. You will realize more of your goals, and you will have the peace of mind that comes with responsible money management. You will be glad you did it.

## How to Use This Book

To get the most from this book it is important to take your time and complete each chapter before moving on to the next. This means that you will be filling out forms, taking quizzes, making calculations, and performing various tasks as you go along. It is helpful if you and your partner work together. In fact, many tasks will require both of you to participate.

The best approach is to read the book a chapter or two at a time. Perform the suggested tasks and then give yourselves some time to think about the results. Each chapter builds on the previous chapters so it's important to read them in order and not to skip ahead. The entire process may take a few weeks but it is well worth your time.

Let's get started.

Kaycee W. Krysty

Kristianne Blake

# About the Authors

## Kaycee W. Krysty

*Kaycee W. Krysty is presently the Director of Personal Finance for the Seattle office of one of the nation's top twenty Certified Public Accountant firms. For the past eleven years, she has successfully helped people develop their own strategies to achieve the personal financial success they desire. She is both a Certified Public Accountant and a Certified Financial Planner.*

*Currently, Kaycee is actively involved to increase the public's awareness about matters that influence their personal finances. Kaycee acts as a special consultant for a Seattle television station on subjects relating to personal finance. And she is a regular featured columnist for a local business publication.*

*Kaycee graduated from Colorado College and attended the University of Denver. She now lives in Seattle with her husband, Michael.*

## Kristianne Blake

*Kristianne Blake, both a Certified Public Accountant and Certified Financial Planner, currently manages her own accounting and financial planning practice in Spokane, Washington.*

*For over 14 years, she has actively assisted individuals and couples in matters such as personal financial planning, estate & trust planning, retirement planning, compensation negotiations and divorce settlements. Kristi is a nationally-recognized speaker and a published author on financial planning topics.*

*Kristi previously was a partner an international accounting firm where she served as Regional Director for Executive Financial Counseling Services in San Diego and Dallas.*

*She received her degree from the University of Washington. Today, Kristi lives in Spokane with her husband, John, and her daughter, Kerry.*

*xiii*

Chapter One
# Do You Fight About Money?

"*Whenever we talk about money for more than five minutes one of us ends up stomping out of the room.*"

"*We know we should be saving money, but somehow the end of the month comes and there is never anything left to save.*"

"*We can't seem to agree on anything about money.....how to spend it, how to save it, where to put it— anything! So we just avoid talking about it all together.*"

"*We are making a lot of money, more money than our parents ever dreamed about, but we just can't ever seem to make ends meet.*"

"*We are in debt up to our eyeballs. We can't even figure out how to get out of debt let alone save any money for the future.*"

If any of the above statements sound familiar, take comfort in the fact that you have lots of company. Many couples, even those with sizable incomes, have these same problems. They may be making lots of money, in fact in 1987 over 18.5% of households in the United States had household income of $50,000 or more. But they are not keeping it. In the same year our national savings rate hit an all time low of 3.2%. And to make matters worse, consumer debt rose to an unprecedented level. What this means is that many couples are slowly bankrupting themselves. Even taking in a comfortable income, by the use of credit they continue to spend more than they earn.

If you are one of these couples you have a problem.

The economic times are uncertain at best. Within recent memory we have seen double digit inflation and a severe recession. The structure and fabric of the U. S. economy is changing before our eyes into a globalized economy governed by factors we cannot control. Our population is rapidly aging; in fact by 1993 , one in four Americans will be 50 or older. And despite our lip service to the American dream, 95% of all Americans reach age 65 at or below the poverty line.

All of these factors point to a need as never before for Americans to take charge of their finances, to act responsibly by saving and investing wisely, and to protect their financial future. Yet it is not happening. Why?

## WHAT'S THE PROBLEM?

First of all, most people are woefully uninformed about personal finance. Even those of us with fancy degrees discover that the business of personal finance is different from any other business situation we may have encountered. To be successful in personal finance requires some knowledge of fundamental principles.

And to compound the problem, there is the strong taboo in our society that forbids discussing finances. Americans don't talk about money; it's "not nice". We think of those who do talk about money as vulgar or crass. For couples, this can be particularly disastrous. Money gets spent with little or no thought as to what for or why. And money once spent will never come your way again.

Even couples who obtain good information about personal finances and break down the barriers to discussing money with each other may not be ultimately successful. To gain knowledge and act upon it requires self-discipline. And getting two people to be self-disciplined at the same time can be a tall chore.

## WHAT MAKES A DIFFERENCE

Those couples who are financially successful in spite of the statistics have found ways to create the self-discipline they need. Typically they have discovered that joint financial success requires good **communication** about money. Good communication implies that they talk regularly about financial matters and that their communication is a two-way street. They listen to one another as much as they talk.

Secondly, they have made a **commitment** to their financial success. Commitment results from reaching some joint conclusions about their financial future that both can embrace wholeheartedly.

The combination of **communication** and **commitment** engenders mutuality in which they as a couple have created and are committed to a vision of the future that reflects their joint objectives.

Finally, to transform **communication** and **commitment** into financial reality requires **cash**. Financially successful couples systematically capture the cash that comes their way and use it to enhance their financial future.

If you want to be one of those couples who beat the odds and become financially successful, you need to do the same thing.

## How This Book Will Help

The techniques in this book focus on the three components of joint financial success:

**Communication**
**Commitment**
**Cash**

In the chapters that follow you will do exercises to get you thinking and talking about money, set goals and negotiate priorities, make a commitment to a joint financial future, and learn an easy and effective method for controlling your cash flow. And following the program in this book can take remarkably little time. You can stop fighting about money and start making it work for you sooner than you think.

The choice is yours. You can choose to be part of the statistics that show that American couples are gradually losing their buying power. Or you can learn to use **communication**, **commitment** and **cash** to achieve the financial success that you desire.

*Chapter Two*
# Why Do You Fight About Money?

Fighting about money is a common area of discord for couples. If you fight about money you are not unusual. Sometimes you will find that your arguments are not about money at all but about other areas of disagreement within your relationship masquerading as financial issues. Yet perhaps more often the friction has at its source some basic differences in style or philosophy about money between the two of you that is fundamental. Or perhaps you don't fight about money at all, in fact you never even talk about it. In either case you as a couple are failing in effective communication about money matters.

To understand why this occurs it is essential to explore what your individual needs and attitudes. Knowing your basic needs and attitudes will help you recognize opportunities for dissent as well as

areas of agreement where you can work effectively together for better results.

## RECOGNIZING DIFFERENT NEEDS

All human beings have differing needs. Satisfying these needs is the strongest known motiva-
tor of human action. Certainly everyone needs the
basics of food, clothing and shelter, but once those
needs are satisfied, other needs demand attention.
Some people have a high need for security, to be
safe and secure from want or peril. Some have a
need for affection, to feel they belong, to receive
affection and love. Others are more concerned
with esteem, they need prestige and the respect of
others. And some need primarily to reach their
own potential.

Most individuals, and probably both of you,
are motivated by some combination of these needs.
Typically you may be more motivated by one
need but you will be motivated to a certain degree
by all of them. Since money is a primary way to
satisfy many needs, conflicting needs between the
two of you can be the source of arguments.

### NEEDS THAT MOTIVATE

| | |
|---|---|
| Physical | to have food, shelter and clothing |
| Security | to be safe and secure |
| Affiliation | to belong, to gain affection and love |

| | |
|---|---|
| Esteem | to have the respect of others, to gain prestige |
| Self Actualization | to do things to reach your own potential |

Perhaps you are considering purchasing a new car. Your current car is still running well but it's not very up to date. It has a few scratches, a loose knob or two, and you're bored with it. The needs that motivate each of you in considering this possible purchase will determine if you think that a new car purchase is wise at this time.

If you are motivated by physical needs, the current car is probably satisfactory. After all, your physical need is for transportation and this car does that just fine. Who needs a new one?

If security is a primary motivation for you , you may only be concerned about safety. Is the current car safe? Or you may be concerned about financial security. You may need to borrow to pay for a new car. Would the car payment be too much?

If affection is your greatest need, you might not care about the car at all. You are primarily concerned about keeping your partner happy in the relationship. If he or she wants a new car, then that's all right with you.

If a need for esteem drives you, you may have a strong desire to purchase a new car. What will people think about you if you are seen in that old beater?

If your strongest need is self-actualization, that is ,the need to reach your potential, you will be primarily interested in how the car can help you do that. Does it go fast enough? Maneuver well?

Obviously, satisfying these differing needs can put you and your partner in direct opposition to each other. Knowing what each other needs provides a basis for communication and compromise.

At the end of this chapter is a quiz regarding needs and motivation: the Motivation Self Analysis Quiz. There are two score sheets so each of you can take the quiz and compare notes. This quiz will indicate what needs motivate you and to what extent. You will be able to spot how differing needs may cause a conflict about money.

### ATTITUDES

Your attitudes can create conflict about money. Your attitude about the ownership of money is particularly critical. Whose money is it anyway? Who earns it? Who spends it? Who pays the bills? Who buys the groceries? Who has the "right" to make the financial decisions? You might be surprised to find that your spouse has a markedly different view of this than you do.

### YOURS AND MINE? OR OURS?

Typically, as a couple you approach your finances in one of two basic ways, either with a *yours and mine* or an *ours* attitude. Your attitude may have nothing to do with legal ownership of money or assets. If your attitude fits into the *yours and mine* category, you believe that each of you should make your own separate decisions regarding the spending or investing of your earnings. If you have an *ours* attitude, you believe that decisions regarding almost all financial matters should be made on a joint basis.

## Yours and Mine

If you share a *yours and mine* attitude toward your money, each of you sets your own goals regarding your own financial future. You individually make decisions regarding your own discretionary money. How will you spend it and on what? When will you invest it and how? However, joint decisions are probably made regarding the shared living expenses and how much each of you contributes to these expenses.

The *yours and mine* attitude toward money is characteristic of couples who share living expenses without a financial commitment to the future. It is also common when the partners involved have divergent financial goals or have incompatible spending behaviors. Also, when either one or both partners have separate financial responsibilities, such as dependents from a previous marriage, this attitude is common.

Couples with the *yours and mine* attitude may end up splitting expenses in a variety of ways:

**The "50/50" or "Roommate Method."** With this method, all expenses are split equally, regardless of differences in income or spending preferences.

**The Relative Income Method.** With this method, he (or she) who has the most, pays the most. If one spouse earns 60% of the income he (or she) pays 60% of the expenses.

**The "Your Kids" Method.** Joint expense are split by either method but when it comes to children of a prior marriage, the birth parent pays 100%.

Any method works as long as both parties are comfortable with it.

## OURS

If you have an *ours* attitude toward your money, you share joint financial goals. Together you make decisions regarding spending and investing. This is not to say that each time a purchase or investment decision is made that both of you must concur. Many spending and investing decisions, which are within the framework of the joint goals, can be made by one of you alone. However, more often than not, you choose to discuss the matter and resolve it jointly. This also does not preclude the availability of some "mad" money for each of you. In fact, some autonomy is essential to making an *ours* attitude work. Many *ours* couples have small separate stashes of money while working as a team with most of their money.

An *ours* attitude is typical when a couple's goals for the future are already similar. When differences occur they are negotiated to reach a compromise. The successful *ours* style requires an ongoing discussion regarding finances so that each partner understands the options available and concurs with each decision.

## HAVING DIFFERENT ATTITUDES

If one of you has a *yours and mine* attitude while the other has an *ours* attitude you may have the potential for serious conflict.

Read the following exercise and discuss your response with each other:

> You are at home on a weeknight waiting for your partner to come home. It is later than usual and you are a little concerned. Your partner arrives and gives you an energetic hug; "Guess what? I got a $5,000 bonus today and I bought a brand new video system on the way home."

> How do you respond?

While this situation may seem a bit contrived, it will point out if your attitudes are in conflict. Responses to this exercise are often varied. Don't be surprised if one of you says "I'd make you take it back the next day," while the other one says, "You earned the bonus and I'm glad you bought something that you have been wanting." If your attitudes conflict, you will need to reach a resolution to this problem or you will continue to fight about money. It is essential to reach a compromise. For example, the partner that has the *yours and mine* attitude might be allowed to make solo decisions about spending and investing below a certain dollar amount. All other decisions would be made jointly. You need to come up with a solution that you both can support.

Functionally, couples who tend more toward *ours* in their attitude seem to have more success in reaching their goals. As in any endeavor, two heads - and two wills - working together are far better than one. If you have not considered taking an *ours* approach to financial management, seriously consider it. A commitment to joint decision making is important in making financial goals a reality.

## Know and Value Your Differences

If you are like most couples, you know that there are elements of opposites attracting in your relationship. Different personalities have different viewpoints on what the future should bring. When you talk about money, differences become apparent.

It is an unusual couple that has no major conflicts of needs or attitudes. The important thing is for you to recognize the differences between you and to value them as a part of what makes each of you unique. You can use this knowledge of why conflict has occurred as a powerful tool to avoid more conflict in the future.

## MOTIVATION SELF-ANALYSIS QUIZ

Here are ten sets of five statements each. Within each set, decide how you feel about each statement in relation to the others.

You are allowed five points for each set, which you can distribute among the five statements depending on the degree to which you agree with the statements.

For example, if you strongly agree with a statement, you can score as high as five points for that statement and nothing for the remaining statements. However, in most sets, you will probably distribute the five points among several statements. Do not exceed the limit of five points for each set.

Write your points in the appropriate columns on the score sheet that follows the quiz. After you have completed the quiz, add up the points in each column to determine your score.

1.   A. I wish I had more pep and energy.

     B. I don't like to move around from place to place.

     C. The greatest things in my life are the love of my family and the respect of my friends.

     D. I enjoy being the "life of the party".

     E. In games, I care a great deal whether I win or lose.

2.  A.  If I didn't have to eat or pay the rent, I probably wouldn't work as hard.

    B.  I want to stay in one location and build for the future.

    C.  I like to join country clubs, luncheon clubs, etc.

    D.  I probably spend more for my car, home, and clothes than my income warrants.

    E.  I enjoy doing a job well, whether or not there is a reward.

3.  A.  The worst thing that could happen to me is to go hungry.

    B.  I like firm and strict supervision.

    C.  I have many friends.

    D.  Among my friends are some of the more influential members of the community.

    E.  I tend to work fast so that I can move on to other opportunities.

4.  A.  I see a doctor regularly and watch my physical condition.

    B.  I wish I had a better retirement plan.

    C.  I do not like being alone.

    D.  If I can't get recognition for a job well done, I'm not much interested in doing it.

    E.  I openly discuss differences of opinion.

5.  A.  I am concerned when I get less than eight hours of sleep.

    B.  I work for accuracy rather than speed.

    C.  I sometimes do what is pleasing to my family and friends even when I want to do something else.

      D. I am talkative even around strangers.

      E. I get great personal satisfaction from a job well done.

6.   A. I wish that I had more time to exercise and keep in top physical condition.

      B. I always prepare for a "rainy day."

      C. My partner, family, or friends have greatly influenced my life.

      D. I would enjoy being referred to as an "ace" in my profession.

      E. My goals are pretty will firmed up for the years ahead.

7.   A. My work is so hectic that I can't eat or sleep as I should.

      B. I think things through very carefully.

      C. I find it difficult to say "no" to a polite and friendly salesperson.

      D. I feel uncomfortable in inexpensive clothes.

      E. I am constantly trying to improve my knowledge and skills.

8.   A. I feel happiest when I am at home.

      B. I like strong leadership.

      C. I try to always understand the feelings of others.

      D. I like to regard myself as a very effective person.

      E. Moving up in an organization is the important thing — the rewards will follow.

9.   A. Most trouble in the world could be overcome

if people had enough to eat and adequate housing.

B. I get a good feeling by having a sizeable savings account.

C. I sometimes color the truth to avoid hard feelings.

D. I'd like to have my associates think of me as an effective person.

E. I sometimes do what I think is best even if others disagree.

10. A. If people have inadequate food, housing and clothing, it's all right for them to resort to violence.

B. I usually side with the majority opinion.

C. I would rather work with someone than work alone.

D. I enjoy winning, especially when the victory is recognized by my friends.

E. There are many important things I want to achieve in my lifetime.

# MOTIVATION SELF-ANALYSIS QUIZ

## HIS SCORE SHEET

|       | A    | B    | C    | D    | E    |
|-------|------|------|------|------|------|
| 1.    | ____ | ____ | ____ | ____ | ____ |
| 2.    | ____ | ____ | ____ | ____ | ____ |
| 3.    | ____ | ____ | ____ | ____ | ____ |
| 4.    | ____ | ____ | ____ | ____ | ____ |
| 5.    | ____ | ____ | ____ | ____ | ____ |
| 6.    | ____ | ____ | ____ | ____ | ____ |
| 7.    | ____ | ____ | ____ | ____ | ____ |
| 8.    | ____ | ____ | ____ | ____ | ____ |
| 9.    | ____ | ____ | ____ | ____ | ____ |
| 10.   | ____ | ____ | ____ | ____ | ____ |
|       |      |      |      |      |      |
| Total | ____ | ____ | ____ | ____ | ____ |

# MOTIVATION SELF-ANALYSIS QUIZ

## HER SCORE SHEET

|      | A | B | C | D | E |
|------|---|---|---|---|---|
| 1.   | ___ | ___ | ___ | ___ | ___ |
| 2.   | ___ | ___ | ___ | ___ | ___ |
| 3.   | ___ | ___ | ___ | ___ | ___ |
| 4.   | ___ | ___ | ___ | ___ | ___ |
| 5.   | ___ | ___ | ___ | ___ | ___ |
| 6.   | ___ | ___ | ___ | ___ | ___ |
| 7.   | ___ | ___ | ___ | ___ | ___ |
| 8.   | ___ | ___ | ___ | ___ | ___ |
| 9.   | ___ | ___ | ___ | ___ | ___ |
| 10.  | ___ | ___ | ___ | ___ | ___ |
| Total | ___ | ___ | ___ | ___ | ___ |

# MOTIVATION SELF-ANALYSIS QUIZ

## SCORING

*Enter below the scores from your score sheets.*

|  | His Score | Her Score |
|---|---|---|

A.  Physical Needs:

The degree to which you are
motivated to satisfy personal
needs (food, shelter, clothing).

B.  Security Needs:

The degree to which you are
motivated to satisfy security
and safety needs.

C.  Affiliation Needs:

The degree to which you are
motivated to satisfy the needs
to belong, to gain affection and love.

D.  Esteem Needs:

The degree to which you are
motivated to gain respect, prestige,
and esteem of others.

E.  Self-Actualization Needs:

The degree to which you are
motivated to reach your potential.

What needs are most important to you?

Compare with the needs of your partner. And remember, no set of needs is superior to any other set!

*Chapter Three*
# Communicating About Money

Fighting about money is a form of communication. But it is the kind of communication that is destructive in making your money work for you. To use communication to improve your personal finances you may need to learn to talk about money in a different way.

You have already looked at some of the needs and attitudes that cause differences between you. Despite those differences you can still learn to communicate more effectively.

In the following chapters you will be asked to share with your partner your thoughts and ideas about your financial future. For this communication to yield long term benefits it is important to be as open and honest as possible. You can expect some differences of opinion. Yet you want to avoid hurting each others feelings.

One way to do this is by using a communication LADDER. This technique is helpful whenever you need to communicate strong feelings to each other. Here's the LADDER:

**L**ook at your rights, desires, needs, and feelings on the matter in advance. Be clear about them and keep them in mind.

**A**rrange a time and place conducive to discussion whenever possible. A planned communication in private goes better.

**D**efine your concerns clearly. Be as simple as possible. Don't make more of the matter than there is.

**D**escribe feelings using "I" messages. These are expressions of feelings that do not accuse or hurt your partner. They don't attack the way a "you" message can.

**E**xpress your request simply and directly. Come right out with what your concerns are. Don't make your partner guess.

**R**einforce cooperation with positive statements. If a difference is resolved in your direction, let your partner know you appreciate it.

Try consciously to use the LADDER techniques if you know you have a tough discussion coming up. By using it consistently, you can gradually make it a permanent part of your communication style.

Your body language while you are communicating with your partner can also affect how you are understood. Try to maintain direct eye contact and erect body posture. Use gestures and facial expressions that are consistent with what you are discussing.

Restate what your partner is telling you. Give him or her the opportunity to confirm the idea that is being communicated. Don't hesitate to use the phrase *"What I thought I heard you say was ...."* Your partner's response lets you know clearly whether or not an effective communication is taking place. Ask your partner to return the courtesy. *"Why don't you restate in your own terms what you think I just said ?"*

Test the waters before you jump into a major issue. Ask your partner open ended questions to get the best sense possible of his or her concern. An open ended question is one which cannot be answered yes or no. It elicits a more complete response. As an example: Ask *"Would you tell me about your wanting a new house?"* instead of *"Do you really want a new house?"*

Becoming aware of your communication style can help you be a more effective communicator. If you are a passive communicator, you may allow other people to take advantage of you. You may let others come first, giving them the message, *"I don't really count."* If you are an aggressive communicator, you tend to overpower other people sometimes by degrading and humiliating them. You always come first, giving the message, *"I'm right and you're wrong."* An effective communication style is a blend of the two. Express yourself freely while respecting the rights and feelings of your partner. Give the message, *"This is what I feel and how I think."*

The key to communication is to *do* it. Even flawed communication is better than no communication at all. If you have not been successful at communicating in the past, *practice* to become a better communicator in the future. Use the exercise at the end of this chapter to share with each other the times that communication is difficult for you.

Make a promise to each other, as you use the techniques in the following chapters, to be on your best and most considerate communication behavior.

## COMMUNICATION EXERCISE

When do you have the most difficulty communicating with your partner?

His    Hers

| His | Hers | |
|---|---|---|
| ____ | ____ | asking for help |
| ____ | ____ | stating a difference of opinion |
| ____ | ____ | speaking up about something that annoys you |
| ____ | ____ | responding to criticism |
| ____ | ____ | saying no |
| ____ | ____ | asking for what you want |
| ____ | ____ | expressing affection |
| ____ | ____ | asking for favors |
| ____ | ____ | expressing disapproval |

What can you do to ease your discomfort?

What can you do to ease your partner's discomfort?

*Chapter Four*
# What Do You Want Your Money to Do For You?

S etting meaningful financial goals is a challenging step in making your money work for you. While some goals are axiomatic, (You do want to send your child to college, don't you?), in the real world of limited resources choices must be made. Because you are a team, you have the added challenge of achieving agreement, that is identifying and ranking goals in a way that you can both support.

The goal setting method suggested in this chapter was developed particularly for couples. It allows each of you to identify goals individually yet to work together to select priorities.

You will have some tough choices to make. Remember to recognize that differences do exist between you. Acknowledge their value to your relationship. These differences may add sizzle to your relationship, keeping it vital over the years. They help to overcome the inevitable familiarity of day-to-day togetherness. Then, you both must be prepared to compromise, which means that each of you *gives* something. Joint financial success is clearly enhanced when you can reach negotiated decisions. Remember the whole is often greater than the sum of its parts. A well-negotiated compromise may prove to be the best possible goal.

## THE NON-STOP

To get started on setting your goals, we offer a writing technique called the "non-stop". This technique allows you to tap your mind and let ideas flow freely and uncensored. Using this technique helps you to uncover goals you might never have considered, goals that never surfaced or that somehow seemed too outlandish. To set goals properly it is essential that all ideas, even silly ones, are discussed and considered. Spend enough time and energy on the non-stop and you may discover some goals which surprise and delight you.

The non-stop technique you will use is based upon discoveries in the last ten years about the differing functions of the right and left hemispheres of the brain. Because of these differing functions, we cannot create and critique at the same time. And our educations have over stressed the critiquing function. The non-stop technique lets the creative part of the brain loose to see where the reaches of our mind might take us. Save for retirement? Maybe. Dream house? Maybe. With the non-stop technique, the only limit to the possibilities are the limits of your imagination.

Here is how the non-stop works. Sit down with a paper and pencil before you. Set a timer for 5 minutes. Pose a question to yourselves and begin writing. Keep writing *without a pause*, even if you write gibberish. As you continue to write your right brain will kick in and ideas, images, and emotions from your subconscious will begin flowing. The non-stop puts you in touch with your more imaginative side.

To begin, practice the non-stop technique by writing about non-financial matters. Ask yourselves questions like "What is my ideal vacation?" or "What would my dream house look like?" This will help you become comfortable with the technique. Then you can use the non-stop technique to specifically formulate your financial goals.

## REACHING BEYOND THE OBVIOUS

If couples are asked to set financial goals without using this technique they often stick totally to the predictable, ignoring new ideas. Or, worse yet, one partner sets the goals and expects the other to fall into line. In both of these situations the couple ultimately fails to reach their goals. Where your goals are only the predictable, there is nothing included that *excites* you. Unless your goals include some element of fun, personal satisfaction, or immediacy, it is unlikely you will stick to your overall financial plan. Where only one partner sets the goals there is no mutual commitment. The other partner often ignores the plan because there is nothing in it for him or her. Why bother doing the tough aspects of financial management if they do not deliver something that each wants?

Consider saving for retirement as an example. It might be twenty years into the future before you will enjoy the fruits of your labor. For most couples, twenty years is a long time to wait. Unless you were both involved in setting the goal and are both committed to it, you may have trouble doing your part to achieve that goal.

Setting your financial goals is an integral part of managing your personal finances. As circumstances change so will your goals. Review your goals periodically to make sure you are going in the right direction.

## GOAL SETTING EXERCISE

It is important to follow these directions as closely as possible. Do not attempt this exercise unless you can set aside an hour or more to actually set some goals for yourselves. To do this exercise you will need:

---

- 2 pads of writing paper

- 2 pens or pencils

- A timer

- Highlighters in 2 colors
  *(optional but highly recommended)*

---

Each of you sit down with your pad of paper in front of you. Sit where you cannot see what the other person is writing. No talking for five minutes, now. No matter how brilliant your idea, wait to share it with your partner until later. Also, if you finish before the timer goes off, leave your partner alone to finish at his or her own pace. Set the timer for five minutes. Begin writing answers to the question, **"What do I want to have/be/do when I grow up?"** Just write. Write without stopping. Write whatever comes into your head. Do not stop to reconsider what you have written. *Just keep writing.*

When the timer goes off, turn your list face down. Do not reread what you have written. Set the timer again for five minutes. Answer the question, **"What do I want to have/be/do now?"** Again, just write. Write fast. Write whatever comes into your head. Do not stop to reconsider what you have written. *Just keep writing.*

When the timer goes off, set this list aside face down. Shake out your writer's cramp and reflect a moment. Did you write anything that surprised you? It is not unusual for an exercise of this type to dredge up some interesting and possibly useful information out of your subconscious.

Now, grab your highlighters (a pencil will do). Agree on colors (or numbers) to represent your priorities:

- Very important
- Somewhat important

At this point, you are still only looking at what you, personally, have written.

Set the timer for two minutes. Look at the list answering, **"What do I want to have/be/do when I grow up?"** Rank these items according to the system you agreed on. For example, if you agreed pink means very important, highlight your very important items with pink and so on. If you cannot immediately categorize an item, move on to something you have strong feelings about and come back to the more neutral item later. You still want to be as spontaneous as possible, so do not slow down. Of course, if a new idea pops into your head, you can add it to the list.

When the timer goes off, set this list aside,

reset the timer and begin on the other list. Use exactly the same procedure. Highlight or number the items according to their importance to you. Do not get bogged down. Keep yourself moving and feel free to add any additional thoughts that come to mind. When the timer goes off again, set your lists aside and take a break, stretch or get a beverage. The best is yet to come.

Now share and analyze what you have written. Trade papers with your partner. Take turns reading the most important items out loud. Remember, your partner is very vulnerable regarding his or her priorities. Ask questions that are non-judgmental. (*"Are you crazy?"* is not an appropriate question.) To get the best understanding of your partner's thoughts, ask questions not requiring "yes" or "no" answers. For example, substitute, *"Why do you want to climb Mt. McKinley?"* or *"Tell me more about climbing Mt. McKinley."* for, *"Do you really want to climb Mt. McKinley?"* The response will be much more revealing.

An important element of goal setting is realizing that you cannot achieve all of your goals. At some point, narrow the focus of the goals you're working toward to increase the chances of actually achieving some of them. For most people, three short-term and three long-term goals are the most that they can keep in mind.

## COMING TO AGREEMENT

Now, here's the tough part. The two of you are going to work to agree to three items from each of the two shared lists to include in your goals. Generally, this is a process of give and take. The six items you choose will form the basis of your formal goals statement.

Use these items to complete the goals statement at the end of this chapter. For your long-term goals, use the three items you selected from the "When I grow up" list. Rewrite each item as required in order to complete the sentence, "In the long run we..." Be as specific as possible. If you can, rank each of the three items in order of importance to you, with the most important first.

Do exactly the same thing with the items you chose from the "now" lists. Take your time. Be as specific as possible. Use positive, action-oriented words. Say "will" instead of "should". *Shoulds* frequently do not happen. We resent being bossed around.

When your goals statement is done, put it away for 24 hours but not more than a week. Then pull the statement out to read it again. Do both of you have a feeling of comfort with, and commitment to the goals when you reread them? Do they feel familiar, as if they belong to you? If not, you may need to do the exercise again. Don't be discouraged. If you are not accustomed to setting goals, it may take time to come up with a statement that feels comfortable. Keep at it. It **will** come. Remember that both of you will grow and change and that your goals statement needs to grow and change with you. Your goals are not cast in stone.

When you complete the goals statement, keep it with your financial records. Refer to it frequently and set a date for updating it. We recommend that, at the very least, you update your goals statement annually. A six-month update is ideal. January is a great month for re-evaluations of every kind. But set a date.

You might be interested in comparing your goals with those commonly written by couples planning their financial future. At the end of this chapter is a Financial Goals Evaluation checklist. Complete this checklist and then compare results. It will give you some insight into your specific financial priorities. This checklist is no substitute for your own goals statement however. Your goals statement probably includes at least a few goals which are not financial, such as - "stay healthy" or "spend more time with the kids." Even though these goals don't appear to be money related they really are. Ultimately all choices you make regarding your time, energy, and resources will have a financial impact. Also, don't be concerned if the checklist uncovers something that you haven't considered. That is what it's supposed to do. Use the results to be sure your goals statement isn't missing an important element. However, don't loose sight of the goals and priorities that you established during the goal setting process; they are unique to you and reflect your fundamental beliefs and values.

## GOALS ARE ESSENTIAL

Making your money work for you takes commitment. By setting goals you have committed yourselves. You have established a reason for getting organized and sticking to a plan of action. And by setting goals carefully and together, you are laying a firm foundation for achieving them.

## GOALS STATEMENT

In the long run we...

1. _____
   _____
   _____

2. _____
   _____
   _____

3. _____
   _____
   _____

Now we...

1. _____
   _____
   _____

2. _____
   _____
   _____

3. _____
   _____
   _____

## FINANCIAL GOALS EVALUATION

Now that you have set your goals, you may
want to compare them with goals which are
commonly set by others. Listed on the following pages are some common financial goals.
Use this list as a check to see that you have included all important matters in your goals.
Indicate the relative importance you attach to
each goal shown by circling the appropriate
number. Try to be realistic and deal with
those goals you truly believe are achievable.
Share your results with your partner. Use the
results to be sure that your goals statement
isn't missing an important element.

## IMPORTANCE TO HIM

Low    High

0 1 2 3 4    Maintain current standard of living

0 1 2 3 4    Improve current standard of living

0 1 2 3 4    Improve future standard of living

0 1 2 3 4    Retire completely at age ____

0 1 2 3 4    Retire partially at age ____

0 1 2 3 4    Provide college education for children

0 1 2 3 4    Accumulate wealth to distribute to heirs

0 1 2 3 4    Support political or philanthropic causes

0 1 2 3 4    Change or modify work situation

0 1 2 3 4    Pursue family activities

0 1 2 3 4    Pursue social activities

0 1 2 3 4    Pursue other personal activities

0 1 2 3 4    Save regularly

0 1 2 3 4    Have peace of mind regarding finance

0 1 2 3 4    Protect against financial loss

0 1 2 3 4    Support adult children

0 1 2 3 4    Support child/adult child with special needs

0 1 2 3 4    Support parents or parents-in-law

0 1 2 3 4    Support surviving spouse

## IMPORTANCE TO HER

Low    High

0 1 2 3 4    Maintain current standard of living

0 1 2 3 4    Improve current standard of living

0 1 2 3 4    Improve future standard of living

0 1 2 3 4    Retire completely at age ____

0 1 2 3 4    Retire partially at age ____

0 1 2 3 4    Provide college education for children

0 1 2 3 4    Accumulate wealth to distribute to heirs

0 1 2 3 4    Support political or philanthropic causes

0 1 2 3 4    Change or modify work situation

0 1 2 3 4    Pursue family activities

0 1 2 3 4    Pursue social activities

0 1 2 3 4    Pursue other personal activities

0 1 2 3 4    Save regularly

0 1 2 3 4    Have peace of mind regarding finance

0 1 2 3 4    Protect against financial loss

0 1 2 3 4    Support adult children

0 1 2 3 4    Support child/adult child with special needs

0 1 2 3 4    Support parents or parents-in-law

0 1 2 3 4    Support surviving spouse

*Chapter Five*
# Where Are You Now?

B efore you can take charge of your financial
future you need a clear understanding of where
you are right now. One of the best ways to do this
is to prepare a net worth statement for yourselves.
A net worth statement is a picture of where you
are financially at a given point in time.

Net worth is measured as the excess of all your
assets over all your liabilities. The following
formula represents net worth:

| What You Own | | Assets |
|---|---|---|
| Less: What You Owe | *or* | Less: Liabilities |
| Equals: What You Are Worth | | Equals: Net Worth |

Like a photograph, this will be a financial
picture of you at a moment in time. The instant
time advances the picture will change.

To figure your net worth pick a moment at
which you want to look. A good time to choose as

the date for your net worth statement is the most recent month end.

The worksheet at the end of this chapter will help in calculating your net worth.

### FILLING OUT THE WORKSHEET

With the worksheet in front of you, begin sifting through your records to determine what your assets and liabilities were as of the date you selected. Fill in whatever comes easiest first.

For example, if your mortgage payment book has the current balance of your mortgage listed on each payment coupon, you can easily jot this balance onto your worksheet. Or if you keep a running balance in your checkbook, you can fill in your cash balance quite easily. Do as much as you can to fill in the blanks quickly. After you get your records organized in the next chapter, you may come across additional items to add to your worksheet. For right now you are just getting a quick fix on where you are.

Be careful not to overlook your liabilities. Don't forget past due bills or credit card balances. Remember that this statement is only for your eyes only, and you need the most complete information possible. High credit card balances or the habit of not paying bills when due is important information for you to have about yourselves! Include them.

Don't be discouraged if there are items on the worksheet that don't apply to you. The worksheet was designed to cover many possibilities. It doesn't mean that you are expected to have entries for every category.

## DETERMINING "FAIR MARKET" VALUE

On your net worth statement show your assets at their "fair market" value. This is the theoretical value at which the asset would be sold between a willing buyer and a willing seller. For some assets, like mutual fund shares, stocks, or bonds, you can determine the values from the financial pages of the newspaper. For other assets, like your house, a "guestimate" is in order. Just don't make the mistake of thinking that what you paid for an asset indicates its value. This is particularly true of personal assets like furniture and clothing. Often you would be lucky to sell those items for 25% of what you paid for them. Remember, fair market value is the price at which you could *sell* the asset.

Once you have listed everything you owe and own on the worksheet, do the addition and subtraction necessary to calculate your net worth.

What do you think? Is it positive or negative? Don't be discouraged even if it is negative. The net worth you have calculated is only a starting point. In the future you will use it to determine your progress.

# NET WORTH WORKSHEET

## ASSETS

| *Description* | *Amount* |
|---|---|
| **Checking Accounts** | |
| _____ | $_____ |
| _____ | $_____ |
| **Savings Accounts** | |
| _____ | $_____ |
| _____ | $_____ |
| **Money Market Accounts** | |
| _____ | $_____ |
| _____ | $_____ |
| **Certificates of Deposit** | |
| _____ | $_____ |
| _____ | $_____ |
| **Stocks and Bonds** | |
| _____ | $_____ |
| _____ | $_____ |
| _____ | $_____ |
| _____ | $_____ |
| _____ | $_____ |
| _____ | $_____ |
| **Mutual Funds** | |
| _____ | $_____ |
| _____ | $_____ |
| _____ | $_____ |
| _____ | $_____ |
| **Other Investments** | |
| _____ | $_____ |
| _____ | $_____ |
| _____ | $_____ |

Cash Value of Life Insurance *(amount you would receive if you cancelled the policy, not the death benefit)*

_____ $_____

_____ $_____

Retirement Accounts *(IRA, Keogh, SEP, Profit Sharing)*

_____ $_____

_____ $_____

_____ $_____

_____ $_____

Real Estate *(Other than personal residences)*

_____ $_____

_____ $_____

Partnerships

_____ $_____

_____ $_____

Business Assets

_____ $_____

_____ $_____

Personal Assets

Residence......................................... $_____

Jewelry, Collectibles, Antiques, etc......... $_____

Automobiles, boats, etc............................ $_____

Household goods..................................... $_____

Other................................................ $_____

(A)  TOTAL ASSETS              $_____

## LIABILITIES

| Description | Interest Rate | Amount |
|---|---|---|
| **Credit Cards** | | |
| | | $_____ |
| | | $_____ |
| | | $_____ |
| | | $_____ |
| | | $_____ |
| | | $_____ |
| **Personal Lines of Credit** | | |
| | | $_____ |
| | | $_____ |
| **Installment Loans Payable** | | |
| | | $_____ |
| | | $_____ |
| | | $_____ |
| **Investment Debt** | | |
| | | $_____ |
| | | $_____ |
| | | $_____ |
| **Personal Mortgage Debt** | | |
| | | $_____ |
| | | $_____ |

(B) TOTAL LIABILITIES          $_____

(C) NET WORTH    (A-B)          $_____

*Chapter Six*
# Putting Your House in Order

Y ou want to make your money work for you. To do that, you need to manage your money as *easily* as possible. This requires organization. Realistically, getting your money life organized takes some time and energy up front. And know how, which is what this chapter provides. Once you are organized, you will find yourselves spending an amazingly small amount of time to keep things on track.

*Hint: Send the kids to the sitter, turn off the phone and spend an afternoon or evening working on this together.*

## YOUR HOME OFFICE

The first thing you need is an environment that is conducive to getting things done, such as an area of your home where you can store and access your financial records easily. Ideally, you should be able to work on your records comfortably in the same location as you store them. Be realistic! If it's a hassle to get at your records, you will not do what is needed to maintain them. So make it easy for yourself to do a good job.

You need some basic equipment in your office. First, you need a file drawer. For most couples, one of those portable file boxes is adequate. Plan to have the entire file devoted to your financial affairs. Also, get plenty of file folders. For easy information retrieval, clearly mark and order your files.

### Shopping List

- Filing Box
- 8 1/2 x 11 file folders *(plenty)*
- Envelopes
- Marking pen
- Shoe box
- Calculator
- File dividers *(6 or more)*
- Stapler
- Pencils

Buy a decent calculator. Contrary to popular belief, a little credit card calculator carried at all times is *not* the key to financial success; an office-size calculator with a real 10-key pad and a tape is. You'll need to add quickly and to check your work. The real thing is indispensable.

*Hint: It's easy to learn to use a "10-key" as rapidly as a grocery store clerk. Just remember to rest the middle three fingers of your hand on the "4-5-6" line of the pad. The "5" has a bump on it to let your middle finger know when it is home.*

## BEGINNING TO FILE

To begin filing, refer to your net worth statement. As previously noted, your statement lists assets in order of *liquidity*. A *liquid* asset is one that can be spent easily. On your net worth statement the most liquid assets are listed first, your least liquid assets last. Liabilities are shown in a very similar way. Liabilities that must be paid soonest are listed first, liabilities that come later are last. Your filing system will follow the same pattern.

First, get out the file dividers. You will use these to create major divisions within your file drawer. Label the dividers as follows:

- Current Items
- Assets
- Liabilities
- Taxes
- Insurance
- Personal

*Place these dividers in the file drawer or box.*

For the current section, label four file folders as follows:

- Goals Statements
- Bills to Pay
- Pending
- Net Worth

Put a copy of your goals statement in the first folder. Keep your net worth statement out for the time being. Put these folders in the first division, *Current Items*.

We'll show you the use of the *Bills to Pay* and *Pending* folders later.

## ASSETS AND LIABILITIES

For the *Assets* division, begin labeling folders in the order the items appear on your net worth statement. You should have a folder for each of your checking accounts, etc. If you hold several investments within a brokerage account you may not need a separate file for each investment. A folder labeled with the name of the brokerage firm may be sufficient. When the folders are labeled, place them in the second division.

Do the same things for the *Liabilities* division. Label the folders in the order they appear on the statement. Be sure there is a folder for every item, e.g. do not lump credit cards together. Have a folder for each card. Or, if you have both a first and a second mortgage on your house, make sure there is a folder for each debt. Place these folders in the third division.

While preparing your net worth statement, you may have unearthed a lot of data which needs to be filed in your assets and liabilities divisions . If you are like most couples, this data was previously stored in nooks and crannies all over the house. You are now going to consolidate that data in one central and accessible location. Go ahead and file things in the logical folders. Do not hesitate to discard useless or repetitive information. For example, get rid of old utility bills, or grocery store receipts. You won't need them.

Any credit card receipt more than 12 months old can probably be tossed, unless it has information that will be used in preparation of your tax return. Then keep it for three years. Remember that too much paper makes files unwieldy so throw things out accordingly.

Here are detailed guidelines on a number of common items:

**Checking Accounts** — You will want the most recent bank statements and check register easily accessible. As it happens, canceled checks fit perfectly in an ordinary shoe box. After reconciling your monthly statement, place the checks in a shoe box and the statement in the file folder. At December 31, each year move the statements and canceled checks to permanent storage. If your bank does not return the canceled checks, you may dispense with the shoe box altogether.

**Other Bank Accounts** — The bank will provide monthly or quarterly statements of your account. Keep the statements in your file folder. At December 31, staple the statements together and move to permanent storage.

**Brokerage House Accounts** — If you have investments held by your brokerage firm, your brokerage statement summarizes your holdings and earnings. Keep the most recent 12 months of statements in your file. After December 31, place the annual summary statement in permanent storage. Discard other statements.

Confirmations of transactions are another matter. Save them with the statements throughout the year (one copy only, typically the broker provides several). At year end, they should be permanently stored with the annual statement. Confirmations are your best source of cost and sales information for tax purposes and should be treated accordingly. If you are doing a lot of trading in individual securities, consider investing in a computerized tracking system.

**Mutual Fund Accounts** — You will receive cumulative statements, i.e. statements that show all your activities year-to-date. Check to be certain they are correct, then toss any preceding statement. At year end, move the statement summarizing the entire year to your permanent file.

*Hint: Do not rely on brokerage or mutual fund statements to correctly reflect transactions. Check them each time you receive one. This can save you much money and heartache later on.*

**Other Securities** — Do *not* keep actual securities (stock certificates or bearer bonds, etc.) at home. They belong in a safe deposit box. Do keep a list of the description and the location of the security. Also, keep any records showing how and when you acquired the security and what your cost was.

**IRAs** — Keep track of your individual retirement accounts by institution *and* individual. If you have two IRAs at Bay National Bank, have a file folder for each one. Keep the monthly statements throughout the year. You should receive a summary statement as of December 31 each year. If so, all other interim statements may be discarded and the annual summary retained for permanent storage.

**Other Retirement Plans** — If you participate in other retirement plans, you will receive, at least annually, a statement of your account. Keep these statements and, at year end, retain the one with the most meaningful date (probably your company's year end). You should have also received a description of the retirement plan and its benefits. Retain this permanently in this folder.

**Your Home** — Place a copy of the settlement sheet from your home purchase in your file. Your title insurance policy should be in your safe deposit box. If you have made any improvements to the home, records of dates and costs should be in this file. Your property tax assessments also go here.

**Other Real Estate** — If you directly own rental properties or other real estate, you will need to keep more specialized records. Most successful real estate investors keep a full set of accounting books.  If you have properties other than your home, you should consider this.

**Jewelry, Collectibles, Antiques** — Prepare a folder for these items and include purchase records of any significant items you already own.  As you make other purchases of these items, put receipts in the folders for cost records.  If the folders become bulky, summarize the receipts and move them to permanent storage.

**Automobiles** — Keep car ownership information and service records on a car-by-car basis.

**Other Assets** — Make folders for other assets you want to track.  Put records in the folders during the year.  At year end, retain only those records that you believe are of permanent importance.  Toss the rest.

**Credit Cards** — For each card, file all receipts as charges are made.  As monthly statements are received reconcile them with your receipts.  Receipts can then be discarded unless they are needed for tax purposes in which case they should be filed in your tax file.  At year end, pull the year's statements, staple, and move to permanent storage.  Maintain in the file the credit card number and the phone number to call in case of loss.

**Personal Loans** — Any document reflecting or explaining the loan agreement should be filed. If there is a loan payment book, include it in the file. If monthly statements are rendered, keep those during the year. At year end, determine if statements have any information not retained elsewhere. Make sure you have something reflecting your actual loan balance in permanent storage.

**Auto Lease** — A copy of your lease should be in the file. Remember it is a disguised loan. So include it in the liabilities section of your files.

**Home Mortgage** — Have a folder for each mortgage. File any document detailing the loan or changing the loan, e.g. an explanation of a payment increase due to an increase in homeowner's insurance costs. File annual statements in permanent storage.

**Other Liabilities** — Create folders as needed. File information as needed. Remember to go through the files at the end of the year and to keep only those items of permanent interest.

TAXES

This section will have a varying number of folders depending upon the complexity of your income tax return. The most common ones are:

> Business Expenses
> Charitable Contributions
> Miscellaneous
> Prior-year Returns

After you pay a bill which has tax implications or any time you receive a document with tax implications, you put it in a folder to be considered when preparing your income tax return after December 31. Copies of prior-year returns are kept in the folder so labeled. When in doubt about the category, file an item under miscellaneous. When you put your tax information together after year end, you can sort it all out.

A file for medical expenses is not included above among the tax folders. Under the Tax Reform Act of 1986, medical expenses are only deductible to the extent that they exceed 7.5 percent of your adjusted gross income (AGI). For most people, this eliminates the deduction completely. For example, if your AGI is $25,000 per year, your medical deductions would need to exceed $1,875 after insurance reimbursement before you would deduct anything. This only occurs if you are uninsured, very sick, or have had significant elective medical care.

## INSURANCE

**Automobile, Homeowners, and Personal Liability Policies** — Create a file for each policy. File the copy of the current policy and any correspondence throughout the year. At year end, save only items which detail your policies currently in force.

**Medical Insurance** — File your benefits explanation book and your copy of the policy. If your plan requires you to file for reimbursement, keep an ample supply of claim forms.

**Life Insurance** — Be sure to have a separate file for each policy. Keep the policy, and all correspondence throughout the year. At year end, only retain information which details an increase in your cash surrender value, dividends received, or a basic change in the policy.

## PERSONAL

This section is for all those items of importance that do not seem to fit into the framework previously mentioned. At a minimum there will be a folder for each of you, and one for each child. File memorabilia like newspaper clippings, personal correspondence of note, report cards, etc. At year end, review the contents to decide what items to keep permanently and store them appropriately. Create folders as needs arise. Planning a vacation? Keeping track of restaurants you would like to visit? Use this section in any way that suits your needs.

Just remember to be strict about the annual clean out.

Once you have organized your filing system, you are ready to use your files to control day-to-day financial matters. Here is how ordinary transactions are handled.

### BILLS TO PAY

In your *Bills to Pay* file keep a list of the bills you commonly pay each month and their due dates. As you receive bills in the mail you place them in the *Bills to Pay* file folder. Keep future payments to make in the folder too, such as estimated income tax payments and real estate taxes. At least once per month (preferably twice) review the folder, pay all bills required and file information as needed. Any item requiring an action other than payment is moved to the pending file.

### PENDING

The *Pending* file should also be reviewed at least monthly to determine if any actions need to be taken. The Pending file will have items in it requiring follow-up. Examples include:

- a credit card statement with an erroneous billing on it (you need to write a letter).
- the annual tabs for your car license (you need to put them on the car sometime when it's not raining).
- a request for reimbursement of medical expenses from your insurance company (you need to make sure they send you the money).

- the perfect birthday card you bought for your brother three months ago (you need to send it right before his birthday).

It is helpful to keep a financial calendar for items you must remember throughout the year in the *pending* file as well as an inventory of your important personal papers. Examples of each follow this chapter.

## ANNUAL CLEAN UP

As mentioned in the descriptions of the individual categories, you will need to move items annually to permanent storage. Before moving items to permanent storage, review them to be sure you have all data needed for your personal taxes. Then move things to storage. If possible, a fire-proof file in an out-of-the-way location in your home is ideal for permanent storage, but any arrangement will do. You are not likely to need to see the items ever again barring an IRS examination, lawsuit, or other unpleasantness.

Even permanent storage requires an occasional clean out. Do this at the time of the December 31 purge of your regular files. Guidelines for retaining records are shown on the following page.

---

**How Long Should You Keep Your Records?**

| | |
|---|---|
| Short term (1 to 3 years) | Household Bills |
| | Expired insurance policies |
| | |
| Medium term (4 to 6 years) | Bank statements |
| | Canceled checks and check registers |
| | Cash receipts details |
| | Paid loan documents |
| | |
| Long term (indefinitely) | Receipts for major purchases |
| | Investment Records |
| | Tax Returns and supporting data |
| | Home purchase and home improvement documents |
| | Business or income property documents |
| | Wills and trusts |
| | Gift tax returns |
| | Papers dealing with an inheritance |

---

## FINANCIAL CALENDAR

You should purchase a pocket size calendar each year. Note on it important financial events and keep it in your *Bills to Pay* file. Consider whether or not any of these items apply to you and note them on the calendar.

- estimated tax payments
  (usually 1/15, 4/15, 6/15, and 9/15)

- real estate tax payments
  (usually twice a year)

- insurance payments

- balloon payments on loans

- other non-monthly loan payments

- vacation payments

- pledged charitable contributions

# INVENTORY OF IMPORTANT DOCUMENTS

## KEEP A COPY IN A SAFE PLACE

Check the items applicable to your situation, and identify location of document or indicate that you are unable to locate it. PS means permanent storage, F means day-to-day files, SD means safe deposit.

*Check if Applicable*

|  |  | Location | Unable to Locate |
|---|---|---|---|
| **PERSONAL PAPERS** | | | |
| ___ | Last will and testament/codicils (self) | _____ | _____ |
| ___ | Last will and testament/codicils (partner) | _____ | _____ |
| ___ | Trust agreements/amendments (self) | _____ | _____ |
| ___ | Trust agreements/amendments (partner) | _____ | _____ |
| ___ | Prenuptial or postnuptial agreements | _____ | _____ |
| ___ | Separation agreements | _____ | _____ |
| ___ | Decrees of divorce | _____ | _____ |
| **INVESTMENT RECORDS** | | | |
| ___ | Personal financial statements | _____ | _____ |
| | Statements of account: | | |
| ___ | Bank accounts/certificates of deposit | _____ | _____ |
| ___ | Brokerage accounts | _____ | _____ |
| ___ | Mutual fund accounts | _____ | _____ |
| ___ | Loan and mortgage accounts | _____ | _____ |
| ___ | IRA/Keogh/pension accounts | _____ | _____ |
| ___ | Partnership/joint venture agreements | _____ | _____ |
| ___ | Loan and mortgage agreements | _____ | _____ |
| | Investments: | | |
| ___ | Prospectus/offering memoranda | _____ | _____ |
| ___ | Transaction confirmations | _____ | _____ |
| ___ | Inventory/appraisals of personal property | _____ | _____ |
| **TAX RETURNS** | | | |
| | Federal and state income tax | | |
| ___ | 19__, 19__, 19__, 19__ | _____ | _____ |
| ___ | Federal gift/estate tax | _____ | _____ |

**EMPLOYEE BENEFIT RECORDS**

Summary plan descriptions:

___ Group life insurance          _____  _____
___ Group medical/dental insurance  _____  _____
___ Pension/profit sharing plan     _____  _____
___ ESOP/stock option plan          _____  _____
___ Thrift plan                     _____  _____
___ Deferred compensation plan      _____  _____
___ Account statements (for above plans)  _____  _____
___ Beneficiary designations (for above plans)  _____  _____
___ Annual benefits summary         _____  _____
___ IRA plan description            _____  _____
___ Keogh plan description          _____  _____

**INSURANCE POLICIES**

___ Life                            _____  _____
___ Annuities                       _____  _____
___ Disability                      _____  _____
___ Hospitalization/major medical   _____  _____
___ Homeowner/tenant                _____  _____
___ Automobile                      _____  _____
___ Other property                  _____  _____
___ Liability umbrella              _____  _____

**EMPLOYMENT RECORDS**

___ Paycheck stubs
    (with earnings and deductions)  _____  _____
___ Employment contracts            _____  _____

**OTHER**

___ _____      _____  _____
___ _____      _____  _____
___ _____      _____  _____
___ _____      _____  _____
___ _____      _____  _____

## Chapter Seven
# Making a Commitment

The action most often required to reach your financial goals is to save money. Want a new house? Save money for a down payment. Want to put the kids through college? Save money for a college fund. Want a comfortable retirement? Save money to provide income when you quit working. Unfortunately, saving money is very difficult for most couples. It requires a joint commitment.

Saving money is a lot like losing weight. People put themselves on a budget to save money just as they put themselves on a diet to lose weight. But statistics show that *diets do not work*. By the same token, *budgets do not work* for most couples either. Clearly, making the commitment to reach your goals requires choices and probably sacrifices. If a budget will not help you, what can?

Paying for your goals *first*.

Most people calculate amounts available for savings as follows:

Family Income
Less: Taxes
<u>Less: Living expenses</u>
Equals: Amount available for savings

They plan to save whatever is left over. But there never is any left over.

This equation fails to yield savings because of the nature of the term *living expenses*. For most people, living expenses expand to consume all available cash. So, by paying for your living expenses first, you may effectively cancel any savings. Typically, your living expenses inflate to fit the cash available leaving little or nothing available for savings.

Consider this alternative calculation:

Family Income
Less: Taxes
<u>Less: Cost of achieving goals</u>
Equals: Amount available for living expenses

With this equation you pay for your goals first by removing your savings before making cash available for living expenses. Your living expenses may still consume all available cash, but that cash amount will be restricted. Your living expenses deflate to a level which still allows you to save for your goals.

Realistically, your living expenses can only be deflated so far. Big house payments or other fixed costs come into play. Children in the family also restrict your ability to reduce costs. This requires a testing of your goals to determine if they are achievable within your financial constraints. If not your goals may need to be adjusted. But universally everyone can accomplish significant savings by using this technique.

If your goals are correctly set, this equation not only provides a natural limit for your cost of living but also gives you the satisfaction of seeing your highest priorities satisfied. You will achieve your most important goals. Putting this concept to work for you will be the focus of the chapters that follow.

*Chapter Eight*

# Capturing Cash

The front-line of making your money work for you is managing the cash that comes your way. The choices you make about that cash, whether you consume or invest it, will make or break your financial future. Consider this:

*Which of these are you more likely to spend?*

- cash in your pocket
- money in checking
- money in savings
- investments

If you answered cash, join the club! The tendency of most people is to spend the cash that they have in their pocket first. It takes more conscious effort to write a check than to pull cash out of your pocket. Yet the money in your checking account is the next to go. For most of you, dollars in your checking account means dollars to be spent, and your checking account balance hovers around the minimum required. More effort is required to spend money that's in savings. And once money has been invested it is rarely consumed. **If you want to increase your savings you should make it as difficult as possible to spend money.** This simple concept will be the cornerstone of your cash management system.

## HOW IT WORKS

Deposit all of your earnings into an interest bearing bank account or money fund, *not* your checking account. Transfer to your personal checking account(s) only the amount designated for living expenses. Use what remains to build up your emergency fund or to invest to support your goals. The underlying philosophy of this procedure is: Out of sight, out of mind. Truly, money that is not in your checking account balance is out of sight, therefore, it is much less likely to be spent.

You will need several bank accounts to implement this program as shown in the following diagram. A collection account for all deposits, one or more checking accounts for spending, and a side savings account to smooth out your living expenses are required. You will also need an investment account for investing for your future.

Your collection account into which you make *all* deposits should be a market-rate checking account, money market fund, a tax-exempt money market fund, or some other instrument that pays

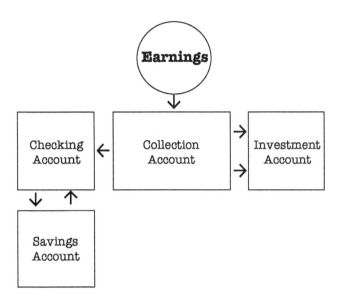

competitive interest rates yet has check-writing or telephone-transfer privileges. A market-rate checking account at a commercial bank or savings and loan probably offers the most advantages: money market interest rates, unlimited check writing (although you may want to consider an account which allows only a limited number of checks per month), government-sponsored insurance on balances up to $100,000, and availability through local banking institutions. The only limitation of most market-rate checking accounts is that they may require a minimum balance of $1,000 to $2,500 and may have a lower after-tax yield than tax-exempt money market mutual funds if you are in the highest tax bracket.

## How to Use Your Accounts

Remember, all of your earnings will be deposited into your collection account. (Note: Earnings do not include investment income. Investment income should be automatically reinvested.) Each month, or more often depending on how often you are paid, you will transfer a set amount to a separate checking account(s) to pay your living expenses.

*Hint: If at all possible, try to keep one joint checking account for living expenses. That way control of spending is focused in one place. However if you need to use two accounts, make sure that you limit the amount transferred into the accounts each month to the set amount for living expenses.*

For funds remaining in the collection account, your first priority is to fund an emergency reserve. Your market-rate account will serve as the investment vehicle for one-half of your emergency reserve. The balance of your emergency reserve will be invested in your investment account. Your emergency reserve is an amount of cash earmarked to tide you over in the event of an emergency. You will need to calculate the necessary amount of your emergency reserve in order to put your cash management system into action. An exercise to help you calculate your reserve is at the end of this chapter.

If the balance in your collection account is less than one-half of your emergency reserve fund requirement, you will not be making any other transfers out of the collection account. Once you have accumulated in your collection account one-half of your emergency reserve, you will begin to transfer amounts into your investment account monthly. In addition to the preset monthly amounts calculated to fund your goals, you will also transfer monthly any amount in excess of the required emergency reserve fund to your investment account.

Once you have deposited the set amount to your checking account to pay your monthly living expenses, this will be all you have to spend for the month. You cannot live beyond this amount by using your credit cards. In fact, if you have a tendency to use your credit cards to live beyond your means, don't use credit cards at all. If large expenditures such as vacations, car insurance, car license, real estate taxes, homeowner's insurance, or a clothes shopping spree make a significant dent in your monthly living on occasion, transfer amounts to your side savings account each month to cover these expenses when they come due.

The side savings account can also be used if you are paid twice a month and your mortgage or rent payment is too large to be absorbed along with your other bills by one-half of your living expense amount. A portion of the living expense amount for the half of the month when the payment is not due should be transferred to the savings account. When the payment is due these funds can be transferred back to the checking account to make the payment.

Your system of accounts and the related transfers are illustrated below:

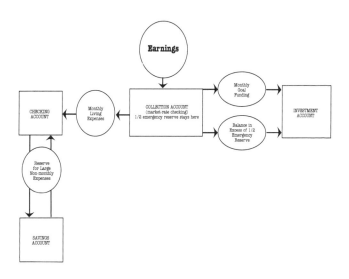

## Choosing A Bank

Your bank can be an important ally in managing your cash. Banks come in all shapes and sizes. The bank that you are using now may not be the best bank for you. The size of the bank may be a factor you want to consider.

Large institutions often have more locations and services than a small bank. They can offer branches throughout the city and the region. If you are a traveler, availability of branches can be important. Large banks also offer a wider variety of services. Determine what services you would use and what they cost.

*Typical Bank Services:*
- varieties of checking and savings accounts
- safe deposit boxes
- automated tellers
- drive-up windows
- notary public
- parking
- loans for cars, boats, home, and businesses
- travelers' checks

## SMALLER MAY BE BETTER

A small bank has different advantages. Being small means each account is a highly-valued asset, and you can expect more personal attention. It is easier to get to know officers at small banks because there is less turnover. Knowing bank officers makes doing business easier. If you establish a good financial relationship with a bank officer, he or she can sometimes bend the rules in your favor.

If you qualify, you can get excellent service from a large bank through their "private" banking department. This is a separate department set up to provide personalized service to affluent customers. Most of these departments will assign an officer to you to assist you with transactions so you are always dealing with the same person.

Ask these questions to determine if a bank is right for you.

- Can you get the type of accounts you need?
- Can you arrange for telephone transfers between accounts?
- Can you pay bills by phone?
- Does the bank offer competitive interest rates ?
- Can you get your salary checks directly deposited?
- Does the bank offer the credit card you want?
- Does the bank offer the services you want?
- Are the bank's fees for services low or non-existent?

A banking relationship is just that — a relationship. If you are happy with your current bank and it meets your needs, stay put.

It will be most convenient for you if your checking account for paying your living expenses and your side savings account are with the same bank or savings association as your market-rate collection account. Some banks allow for telephone transfers between accounts, which would save you at least one trip to the bank each month. Other banks may allow you to have a free checking account with no minimum balance requirement if you also maintain a market-rate account with them.

This cash management system will help you buy your future first. You will accomplish this by making all earnings deposits to a collection account then limiting cash available for living expenses. Buying your future first is also accomplished by building your emergency reserve before making monthly transfers to your investment account where you will invest to achieve your financial goals. Once this money is transferred to investments, it will be even more difficult to spend it on a whim. Getting your money working for you and keeping it working for you is the key to reaching your financial goals.

## EMERGENCY RESERVE CALCULATION

There are several reasonable approaches for determining the amount of cash or its equivalent to have available immediately to meet an emergency. All involve varying degrees of personal and subjective judgments. Some people consider the availability of insurance coverages or loans or lines of credit or credit card borrowing limits when determining the amount of your emergency reserve. However, the one emergency where your personal credit or insurance could evaporate would be loss of your livelihood. While the probability of job loss may be low, its impact on short-term financial well being can be severe. Accordingly, a conservative emergency reserve is desirable.

The standard emergency reserve is six months of income. This is a good place to start, but it is only a start. The concept of income overstates the actual need for a reserve. In a genuine emergency when you live off savings you do not pay taxes or continue to save or invest. Therefore that standard should be discounted to the amount necessary to cover six months net living expenses.

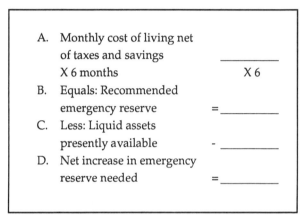

A.  Monthly cost of living net
    of taxes and savings          _____
    X 6 months                      X 6
B.  Equals: Recommended
    emergency reserve             = _____
C.  Less: Liquid assets
    presently available           - _____
D.  Net increase in emergency
    reserve needed                = _____

Only 50 percent of this amount needs to be in the market-rate (collection) account. The rest should be in a liquid investment such as marketable certificates of deposit.

E.  Recommended emergency reserve
    *(Item B. above)*             _____
                                    X 50%
F.  Equals: amount to be maintained
    in the market-rate (collection)
    account                       = _____

*Chapter Nine*
# Paying for Your Goals

C onsider how we have suggested you set up
your banking arrangements: You will have
a collection account where all income is deposited. Once or twice monthly you will transfer a
specified amount to your household checking
account to handle all living expenses. By doing
this you enforce the **buy your future first** disci-
pline. Your monthly savings are being captured
in the market-rate account to be saved and invested. This chapter will help you figure out
exactly how this can work for you.

How much money should you transfer
monthly for living expenses? How much money
should you keep to fund your goals? The worksheet at the end of this chapter will help you
calculate these amounts, just as in the example on
the following page.

**Cash Available for Living Expenses**

| | |
|---|---|
| Monthly Income | $3,200 |
| Less: Taxes | - 786 |
| Monthly Income Net of Taxes | $2,432 |
| Less: Amounts to fund goals | |
| Retirement savings    $270 | |
| Trip to the Olympics  238 | |
| Total for Goal Funding | - 508 |
| Monthly Amount Available for Living | $1,924 |

The first step is to calculate how much money you need to save monthly to pay for each of your goals. List each goal from your goal statement on the Step One worksheet at the end of this chapter. Be careful to list goals as either long term or short term. You will use different methods to quantify the goals depending on whether they are short or long term.

You can easily quantify short term goals. Simply divide the estimated cost by the number of months between now and when you will need the savings. For example, if one of your goals is to buy a house in 5 years (60 months) you might estimate that the down payment and other related cash requirements will be $ 30,000. Then you need to save $ 500 ($ 30,000÷60) each month if you haven't already started saving. If you have already set aside $ 9,000 towards your house purchase, you can reduce your savings to $ 350 ($ 21,000÷60) each month. This approach will also work for goals such as vacations, children's education, and other significant acquisitions. You will note that this approach does not consider possible investment earnings or the effects of inflation on the cost of your goal. This approach will provide you with a simple, straightforward and conservative answer. Leaving investment earnings and inflation out does just that.

Goals such as providing for your family in case of your death or disability can best be met by the purchase of adequate disability and life insurance. The monthly cost of this insurance would be considered the cost to fund the related goal. You may need to consult with an insurance professional to determine the exact monthly cost of your goal.

For long term goals, such as retirement, possible earnings on your investments and the effects of inflation on the cost of your goal need to be considered. Calculating the amount you need to save in order to retire at a specific age is complicated. And given our changing economic environment any assumptions you make when performing the calculation may not hold true over the relatively long time period being considered. We suggest that instead of performing this calculation, you try to save at least the minimum level indicated within the guidelines shown below. This chart estimates the amount that, including the effects of investment earnings and inflation, you need to save monthly in order to have $1,000, $2,000 or $3,000 per month of spendable income at retirement. This would be income above and beyond any pension or Social Security income you may expect. You need to increase the amount you save each month to keep pace with inflation. This adjustment can be made annually. If the guideline amount is more than you can currently afford, strive to save at least some amount each month toward retirement.

### RETIREMENT SAVINGS GUIDELINES

| Years remaining until retirement | If your desired spendable income per month at retirement is: | | |
|---|---|---|---|
| | **$1,000** | **$2,000** | **$3,000** |
| | *Every month you should save at least:* | | |
| 40 | $200-$220 | $400-$440 | $600-$660 |
| 35 | $250-$270 | $500-$540 | $750-$810 |
| 30 | $320-$340 | $640-$680 | $960-$1,020 |
| 25 | $420-$440 | $840-$880 | $1,260-$1,320 |
| 20 | $570-$590 | $1,140-$1,180 | $1,710-$1,770 |
| 15 | $830- $850 | $1,660-$1,700 | $2,490-$2,550 |
| 10 | $1,350-$1,380 | $2,700-$2,760 | $4,050-$4,140 |

*Remember to increase your savings each year by the rate of inflation.*

An example will help make this clear. You would like to retire when the elder of the two of you reaches age 65. The elder is currently 35. Therefore you have 30 years to save for your retirement. The chart assumes that your life expectancy is 20 years after retirement. You estimate that you want at least $2,500 per month of spendable income in today's dollars. You also estimate that your pension plus Social Security will provide at least $1,500 per month after tax in today's dollars. Therefore you need to save enough to provide an additional $1,000 per month of spendable retirement income. If you refer to the guidelines you will find that you need to save $250-$270 per month toward that goal. To keep up with inflation in the following year and each year thereafter you will need to increase your savings by the rate of inflation for that year. If inflation is 5%, you will in increase the amount you save each month by 5%, e.g. $250 becomes $263.

The guidelines assume that your investment returns will exceed the annual rate of inflation by at least 3% after tax. Keep in mind that this is a relatively aggressive assumption; that is, it assumes that you will do well with your investments. Even though 3% may not sound like a lot, on an after-inflation and after-tax basis it is. Consider a certificate of deposit that yields 8% each year. If your tax rate is 30%, your after tax rate of return is reduced to 5.6%. If inflation is 4%, your after tax and after inflation rate of return is only 1.6%. This is much less than the 3% assumed in the guidelines. Since you are saving for retirement be careful not to take unnecessary investment risks with your savings but you will need to take some risk to obtain the necessary returns. Be aware that just saving the money is not enough to assure a comfortable retirement; you must prudently invest the money as well.

## CALCULATING MONTHLY LIVING EXPENSES

Once you have figured out the required monthly savings for each of your goals, you are ready to move to the next step. Step two helps you to calculate exactly how much you will have available to live on after paying your taxes and funding your goals.

Two alternative worksheets appear at the end of this chapter. If you are paid monthly or semi-monthly, use the monthly worksheet. If you are paid on any other basis, such as biweekly, you may want to adjust the worksheet accordingly or use the annual worksheet. If part of your compensation includes an annual bonus you should definitely use the annual worksheet.

The first step in completing the worksheets is to enter your monthly or annual gross income. As an employee this is your total pay before subtracting taxes and any other amounts that may be deducted from your paycheck. Generally the other amounts deducted are part of your living expenses. Any amounts deducted that are contributed to a retirement plan or otherwise invested can be considered as part of your monthly savings towards retirement. This will reduce the amount that is required to be transferred to your investment account for your retirement savings.

Next, subtract taxes. This includes federal and state income taxes and Social Security tax. Generally if you don't owe a lot to the IRS on April 15 or if you don't have a large refund coming, you can make the calculation using the amounts that are subtracted from your paycheck. Otherwise you will need to make an adjustment.

If you are doing the worksheet on an annual basis, you will need to divide your income less taxes by twelve to compute your monthly income net of taxes.

Then, referring back to Step One, enter the monthly amounts needed to fund each of your goals. Add up these amounts to determine the total amount needed each month to fund your goals.

Subtract the total goal funding amount from your monthly income net of taxes. The net result is the amount that you have available for monthly living expenses and should be the amount that you transfer from your collection account to your checking account each month.

When the balance in your market-rate collection account is sufficient to cover one-half of your emergency reserve, you can begin transferring the total amount for goal funding to your investment account each month.

After you have completed the worksheets, consider the result in light of what you know your present cost of living to be. It is important that you set a workable amount.

*Hint: How much money do you presently deposit in your checking account each month? Does it all disappear? That is your present cost of living.*

If the amount you calculate as available for living seems unreasonably small, there are two alternatives for you to consider.

**Reconsider Your Goals** — Occasionally, couples have trouble living on their "amount available for living expenses" because their goals are unreasonably high. If more than 20 percent of your available income is going to fund goals this could be you.

If you think this may be happening, go back to look at your goals. Remember you cannot have it all. Commonly, there are two situations where conflict occurs.

The desire to provide for your children's education may conflict with your desire to retire at an early age because children's educations are so expensive. You may be forced to make some trade-offs. Unless you are at an unusually high income level, providing a college education for your children and having an early retirement may be incompatible goals.

The summer home or boat bind happens because owning a summer home or boat represents a significant outflow of cash that most people cannot afford without giving up another major life goal. To decide whether a summer home or a life goal. To decide whether a summer home or a boat is in your future decide why you want to own one. Couples often say they would rather own than rent so that they will be more likely to use the boat or cabin. But the fact is that most boats are moored 90% of the time and most cabins are empty most of the time. This seems to be a high price to pay for forcing yourselves to vacation.

If forced vacations are your motivation, a better method is to make prepaid reservations for a variety of times throughout the year to charter a boat or rent a summer place that appeals to you. No maintenance is required and the total cost should be significantly less than ownership.

**Make More Money** — You may try to live on the amount you calculated to be available for living expenses and experience genuine frustration. "We cannot do it," you are thinking; "We just cannot live on what is left over after we fund our goals." After reviewing all other alternatives you may still believe that this is the hard truth; your family really cannot live a satisfactory life on the allocated amount of money.

One solution is to make more money.

All jests aside, this may be the most feasible answer. For families who prefer to keep their lifestyles up to a certain level, making more money may be an excellent solution.

How to do it? The most common way is for one partner to work more, to take on a new or extra job, or to start a small business. The disadvantage is that extra costs for child care, taxes, wardrobe, and other items can greatly reduce the amount of additional income you will actually create. Also, the increased strain on time can be a problem. On the other hand, the need to make more money may be just the push one partner needs to get a career started or advanced.

If you think making more money may be the solution for you, consider all the ramifications carefully.

For cash management to be effective, the amount you transfer each month for living expenses must be high enough to be workable. An amount too low encourages breakdown of the barriers that you have raised against spending the savings you have set aside for your goals. But, the amount should not be too high either. Do not miss opportunities to achieve your goals faster if you believe you can reduce your cost of living further. The bottom line is, if you are living well and progressing rapidly toward meeting your goals, you are right on target.

## *STEP ONE*
## SHORT TERM GOALS

Short Term Goal #1

_____

_____

        a.  Amount needed     _____

        b.  Number of months  _____

        c. Monthly amount (a÷b)  _____

Short Term Goal #2

_____

_____

        a.  Amount needed     _____

        b.  Number of months  _____

        c. Monthly amount (a÷b)  _____

Short Term Goal #3

_____

_____

        a.  Amount needed     _____

        b.  Number of months  _____

        c. Monthly amount (a÷b)  _____

## *STEP ONE*
## LONG TERM GOALS

Long Term Goal #1

_____
_____

      a.  Amount needed        _____

      b.  Number of months   _____

      c. Monthly amount (a÷b) _____

Long Term Goal #2

_____
_____

      a.  Amount needed        _____

      b.  Number of months   _____

      c. Monthly amount (a÷b) _____

Long Term Goal #3

_____
_____

      a.  Amount needed   _____

      b.  Number of months   _____

      c. Monthly amount (a÷b) _____

### *STEP TWO*
### CASH AVAILABLE FOR LIVING EXPENSES
### MONTHLY

Monthly Income _____

Less: Taxes (including Social Security) - _____

Monthly Income Net of Taxes = _____

Less: Amount to Fund Goals from Step One

     Short term Goal #1 _____

     Short term Goal #2 _____

     Short term Goal #3 _____

     Long term Goal #1 _____

     Long term Goal #2 _____

     Long term Goal #3 _____

Total for Goal Funding - _____

Monthly Amount Available for Living = _____

*Is this amount realistic?*

*Hint: A goal you can never reach may be worse than no goal at all. Do what you can to be sure that your goals are financially achievable.*

## STEP TWO
## CASH AVAILABLE FOR LIVING EXPENSES
## ANNUAL

Annual Income                                              _____

Less:  Taxes *(including Social Security)*        -      _____

Annual Income Net of Taxes                     =      _____

                                                                ____ ÷ 12

Monthly Income Net of Taxes                   =      _____

Less:  Amount to Fund Goals from Step One

    Short term Goal #1         _____

    Short term Goal #2         _____

    Short term Goal #3         _____

    Long term Goal  #1         _____

    Long term Goal  #2         _____

    Long term Goal  #3         _____

Total for Goal Funding                            -      _____

Monthly Amount Available for Living     =      _____

*Is this amount realistic?*

   *Hint:  A goal you can never reach may be worse than no goal at all.  Do what you can to be sure that your goals are financially achievable.*

*Chapter Ten*
# Wise Use of Credit

W hen used wisely, credit can be a helpful tool in making your money work for you; however, credit can also be dangerous. Without careful consideration it is all too easy to become overextended. For most individuals, credit cards are the major source of individual credit. However, personal lines of credit (PLCs) are becoming increasingly common. This chapter will provide you with specific guidelines for getting your credit under control and keeping it there.

Make it a rule to use credit only to purchase assets of lasting value. That means financing your home and perhaps your car. Make all other purchases with cash unless you can pay the balance in full each month. Properly used, credit cards can provide you with convenience, safety, and float. Your PLC can offer you ready cash when the need arises. But these benefits are costly if your credit gets out of control.

## CREDIT CARDS

**Convenience** — At many stores, it is easier to pay for a purchase with a credit card than a check. If you write a check for a purchase, the store may require a major credit card as a reference or identification. Most businesses will not accept out-of-state checks when you travel. When you are out of the country, you do not need to purchase or carry large amounts of foreign currency if you can use your card. Often the exchange rate given is advantageous.

**Safety** — Credit cards are safer than cash. If your credit card is stolen, there is protection against unauthorized use if you report your card missing. This is particularly valuable when you are traveling and might otherwise be carrying large sums of cash.

**Float** — Your credit cards can be the closest thing you will ever have to free use of money. If you understand the billing cycles and how the finance charges work, you can take advantage of the float by paying the card balance off before any interest is charged.

Proper use of cards is important in establishing your credit rating. Your good credit rating is essential in obtaining home mortgages or business loans.

To be a wise user of your credit cards avoid abusing them. If two or more of the following apply to you, you are probably a credit card abuser:

- Are this month's total credit card balances due larger than last month's balances?

- Do you pay only the minimum payment due or less than the full balance on your credit cards?

- Have you added new credit card accounts in order to increase your borrowing power?

- Have you lost track of how much you owe?

- Do you avoid adding up your total amount due on credit card accounts?

- Are you using credit cards in situations where you used to pay cash?

- Are you using credit card cash advances or checking account credit lines to pay old bills instead of current ones?

- Have you paid off large balances only to run up another large balance very soon thereafter?

- Do you use your credit card to help make ends meet at the end of the month?

- Are your credit card balances increasing only to be stopped when you reach your credit limit?

If you *are* a credit card abuser, the best way to solve your problem is to *quit using your credit cards.* It's simple, cut them in half. If you are not a credit card abuser, but you are currently overextended (not paying your entire credit card balance each month), you do not need to cut your cards in half, but you should put them away for awhile. Your safe deposit box is the best location to store them. Then determine exactly who you owe and how much you owe to develop a strategy for paying these balances off over a reasonable period of time.

## PERSONAL LINES OF CREDIT

Many individuals now have additional borrowing power in the form of a personal line of credit (PLC). This is a flexible arrangement where the lender authorizes a credit limit and then the individual borrows as needed up to that limit. Repayment terms vary; however, most PLCs are usually available at lower interest rates than credit cards.

Unquestionably, a PLC is a great convenience. All of us, occasionally, come face to face with a situation where our need for cash exceeds our cash readily available. But be careful. A PLC can be misused just as easily as a credit card. Consider the same danger signals to determine if you are using or abusing your PLC.

## CREDIT REDUCTION STRATEGY

The first step is to set a specific goal like, "We would like to pay off all our credit cards in 18 months." You then need to quantify this goal in terms of monthly payments. This will allow you to determine if you have set an achievable goal. A calculation of the monthly amount is at the end of this chapter.

After you have determined how much to commit to reducing your credit card debt monthly, you need to rank which debts will be paid off first. Continue making the minimum monthly payments on all of your bills but, beyond that, you have some flexibility. It is possible that the interest rate being charged on each of your debts is different from the others. The debts with the higher interest rates should be paid off first. Your net worth worksheet will indicate which debts have the higher rates.

If you have home equity available to use as a borrowing base, you may wish to use it to pay off your credit card balances once and for all. By doing so, you will at least be making tax deductible interest payments. But use caution. The danger is that you will use an equity loan to pay off current bills then go right out and charge new bills which put you right back in the same situation.

If you are not a credit abuser or not currently overextended, congratulations! You are using your credit wisely. But, be careful. It is easy to fall into the credit abuse trap.

## CREDIT REDUCTION STRATEGY

Personal debt       _____

Desired number of months to pay off    + _____

Monthly payment before interest    = _____

Interest rate adjustor*    X    1.1

Minimum monthly payment to reduce debt   = _____

*Hint: Pay minimum monthly payments first then allocate any excess to the debt with the highest interest rate.*

*This adjustor will approximate additional interest costs.

*Chapter Eleven*
# Home Sweet Home

R enters typically dole out at least 25 percent of their monthly gross income for shelter. Put the same amount toward mortgage payments on your own home and you will be gaining equity, generating tax deductions, and hedging against inflation. For these reasons, owning a home has traditionally been an important goal for most couples. This chapter will suggest ways that home ownership can make your money work for you.

You may already own a home and are currently enjoying some of these financial benefits. If so, you are probably also aware of the hassle of home ownership. But given the opportunity to make the choice again wouldn't you choose home ownership? In fact, many of you may be considering purchasing your second or third home.

There are three crucial aspects of successful

home ownership from a financial perspective: buying the right home, selecting the best financing, and getting the mortgage paid off. This chapter will explain all three.

## THE BUY DECISION

When making the decision to buy a home you need to be fully aware of the total cost associated with the purchase. It is more than the fees or points that the bank or mortgage company charges you on your mortgage. It is more than the cost of physically moving your possessions. There are hidden costs of moving into a new home.

Many homes require some adjustments or remodeling to fit your lifestyle, which can be costly. You need to consider these costs when making the decision to buy a particular home. If you have to sell your present home, you also incur transfer costs like commissions and taxes. Often left out of the equation are the small costs of making the house your home. These costs add up, particularly if you are buying a home for the first time. You will need garbage cans, lawn mowers, hoses, shelf paper, new wallpaper, a fresh coat of paint, new locks on the doors, area rugs for hardwood floors, new curtains, linens to coordinate with your new baths and kitchen. The list goes on. Some experts suggest that you estimate the cost of purchasing and moving into a new home to be at least $15,000 above and beyond the purchase price of the new home itself.

Because of the high cost, buying and moving into a new house is not a decision to make lightly. To justify the up-front costs, plan on living in your home for a minimum of five years. Wise home buying follows the seasons of a couple's life. Most couples will live in their first home for five to ten years. They will live in their second home, or family home, for about twenty years. Then they will be looking for a smaller home to live out their retirement years.

To choose a home properly, visualize what your lifestyle will be like over the time you plan to live in the house so that you can make a wise selection. For example, couples who are planning to have children should choose a home that accommodates the entire family. Somehow that view house on a steep hillside you thought you wanted is not as attractive when you consider a two-year-old falling off the deck. Be practical.

## FINANCING

Buying a home not only involves buying the right house but also finding the right mortgage. Your options for mortgages today are as varied as your choice of homes. The key to getting the mortgage that is right for you is shopping around. Sources of mortgage money include saving and loan associations, savings banks, mutual savings banks, credit unions, commercial banks, mortgage companies, and the seller of the house you want to buy. Not all of these lenders offer all types of mortgages.

The one easy way to shop for a mortgage is to go to a reputable mortgage broker. A mortgage broker is not a lender. The broker is authorized by many different lenders to offer each lender's mortgage programs. Because brokers have a large number of sources available, they can pick and choose among them for the mortgage program that best suits your needs. Brokers are usually paid by the lender and there should be no additional cost to you for using a broker.

Or you can survey the local banks, savings and loans, and mortgage companies to create your own cost comparisons. But the important thing is to shop around. At any point in time lenders in your area may have widely differing terms. Because you will live with your mortgage for a long time, it is essential to get the best terms that you can.

Do not forget the sellers of the home as a possible financing source. They may have an assumable mortgage already on the property or may be willing to finance all or a portion of the mortgage themselves.

## How Much? How Long?

How much should you put down as a down payment and how long should your mortgage term be? This depends on your personal financial situation and on whether this is your first or subsequent house. The general rule for debt is that consumer items such as furniture, cars, boats, etc., should be paid off as soon as possible. However, this should not be done at the cost of depleting your investments and emergency reserve funds. In reality, a house is a type of consumer good and is subject to the same rules. Once other consumer debt is paid, paying down your mortgage can become a priority if appropriate for you.

**First House** — When you buy your first house, you are scraping together every dime you can find to make your down payment. This probably means that you have wiped out all of your liquidity including your emergency fund. These funds need to be restored. They can be restored by saving each month. It will be easier to accomplish this if your mortgage payments are as low as possible. The longer your mortgage term the lower the payments will be. So you need to look for the longest mortgage term available, which will generally be 30 years.

With your first home purchase you will probably not have any choice about the size of your down payment. You will be caught in a bind between how much you have saved for your down payment and how large a monthly payment you can afford to make. You're in a better bargaining position to get a good mortgage deal if your down payment is substantial.

If your down payment is 20 percent or more, you will not have to spend extra money to purchase private mortgage insurance. The purpose of private mortgage insurance (PMI) is to guarantee, if you default on the mortgage payments, that the lender will get back the full balance of the loan. If your down payment is less than 20 percent, your lender will probably require you to purchase PMI. You can pay for PMI either in a lump sum at the time of settlement or monthly. The lump sum payment can be as high as 3.5 percent of the borrowed amount. On a monthly basis, the first year costs approximately five dollars for every thousand dollars of coverage. Since PMI is so expensive try to avoid it if at all possible.

**Subsequent Homes** — When buying subsequent homes use the entire equity in your old home as the down payment on your new home. The ability to use your home equity as a down payment enables you to preserve your existing investments and emergency funds each time you buy a house.

With this home purchase you have more flexibility in deciding how long your mortgage should be. A 15-year mortgage will allow you to pay off your home sooner—at a significantly lower overall cost — than a 30-year mortgage. However, the monthly payments on a 15-year mortgage will be greater.

One way to retain flexibility is to take out a 30-year mortgage and make payments equivalent to what you would have been making if you took out a 15-year mortgage. You will be able to almost pay off the mortgage in 15 years, but if your cash flow is tight for a month or two you can reduce your payment to that required by the 30-year mortgage without penalty.

There is a cost for this flexibility. The interest rates charged for 15-year mortgages are generally lower than the rates charged on 30-year mortgages. Often, this cost is worthwhile if the difference in the rates is .5 percent or less.

**Retirement Home** — The shortest possible mortgage is ideal for your retirement home. When retiring most couples buy a smaller home which is less expensive than their family home. The equity built up in the family home may be enough to fully pay for the retirement home. Otherwise choose a 10- or 15-year payoff.

## FIXED OR ADJUSTABLE RATE?

Choosing between a fixed-rate or an adjustable-rate mortgage is another home-buying decision that you will face. A fixed-rate mortgage is the standard old reliable mortgage that your parents had. Until recently a fixed-rate mortgage was the only kind of mortgage available. In a fixed-rate mortgage, the interest rate is determined at the time the loan is arranged and that rate remains constant throughout the life of the loan. You always know how much your monthly payments will be because they never vary from the first to the last installment. The consistency and the security of knowing exactly how much your payments will be is a significant advantage of the fixed-rate loan.

An adjustable-rate mortgage (ARM) is a mortgage in which an initial interest rate is set at the time the loan is taken out; however, the interest rate is adjusted at fixed intervals during the term of the loan according to a specified formula. The interest rate you pay on your mortgage loan changes periodically based on fluctuations in the general level of interest rates.

Initial interest rates on ARMs tend to be lower than those on fixed-rate loans because with an ARM you assume much of the risk of interest rate fluctuations. Thus, the lender needs less protection against a possible future rise in interest rates.

What type of mortgage loan is best for you? A few years ago, when interest rates were high and on a roller coaster ride, the best advice was to try to get an ARM. Of course, you took the risk that interest rates would move against you. But in return the lender gave you a lower initial interest rate. And when interest rates were at 14 percent or higher, any concession seemed worth a gamble. The same advice no longer holds true today.

Now that interest rates have declined to a level that seems acceptable and reasonable, why take a chance on an ARM? Why bother with indices, margins, and fluctuating payments? The answer is clear. When fixed-rate mortgages are available at reasonable rates, choose a fixed-rate mortgage loan on the best possible terms. When rates are unreasonably high, choose an ARM.

There are a number of fees the mortgage lender may require you or the seller to pay at closing. The most significant of these is "points". Each point represents a one-time charge of 1 percent of the total amount of the mortgage loan. Points may or may not cover specific cost items of the loan. One lender may charge you 10 percent interest and two points on a mortgage while another lender may give you 9.5 percent, but will charge you three points. How do you evaluate which of these is the better deal? The answer to this question depends on how long you intend to keep the home and the related mortgage. The shorter the period you intend to keep the loan the better off you are paying the higher rate of interest and paying the lower points. If you intend to keep your home for a long period of time and if the interest rate differential is great, consider paying the additional points up front.

## ACCELERATING YOUR PAY DOWN

It may be best for you to pay off your mortgage on an accelerated basis. There are several reasons for you to consider this.

**You always need a place to live** – a mortgage-free home can be a powerful asset in reaching early retirement. If you don't have to make mortgage payments, you reduce the amount of spendable income that you need in retirement.

**Interest is expensive, even if it is deductible** – unless you have an old mortgage, the rate of interest that you are paying is probably at least 10 percent. It is difficult to find alternative low risk investments with yields that high. Paying down your mortgage on an accelerated basis is like making a long-term investment at the same yield.

**The cost is low for a big reward** - paying down your mortgage on an accelerated basis can be surprising affordable. Compare payments on a $100,000 mortgage at varying interest rates:

| Interest Rate | 15-year Payment | 30-year Payment | Factor of Increase |
|---|---|---|---|
| 8% | 955.65 | 733.76 | 1.3 |
| 9% | 1014.27 | 804.62 | 1.26 |
| 10% | 1074.61 | 877.57 | 1.22 |
| 11% | 1136.60 | 952.32 | 1.19 |
| 12% | 1200.17 | 1028.61 | 1.17 |

If you cannot presently afford to increase your payment to the 15-year level, much can be achieved by increasing your payment even $50 or $100 per month. For example an increase in the monthly payment of $100 per month on a $100,000 mortgage at 10 percent reduces the paydown from 30 to 19.25 years. Think of it: over ten years with no mortgage payments simply by paying an extra $100 per month now!

At the end this chapter is a quiz which will help you determine if accelerating the paydown on your mortgage is appropriate for you.

## TAXES

Home ownership has always provided special tax benefits.

**Deferred Gains** — If you sell your house at profit, you may be able to avoid paying tax on the gain. In general, no tax is due on the gain if you buy or build a replacement residence within 24 months before or after the sale of the former residence and if the cost of the replacement residence equals or exceeds the adjusted sales price of your old residence. If the new residence costs less than the adjusted sales price of the old residence, any gain on the sale of the old residence is recognized only to the extent of the difference between the two prices. In either case, any gain not recognized is deferred to a later sale by reducing the cost basis of the new residence by that amount.

**Gain Exclusion** — For taxpayers age 55 or older there is an additional tax benefit. If they have used the residence as their principal residence for three out of the five years prior to the sale, up to $125,000 of the gain can be completely excluded from tax. This election is available only once in a taxpayer's lifetime and unused amounts of the exclusion are lost.

**Deduction of Mortgage Interest** — Even with recent changes in the tax law, interest paid on loans to purchase or improve your home remains deductible. In general, you may fully deduct interest paid on all indebtedness incurred to purchase, construct, or substantially improve the home. This is called acquisition indebtedness. After December 31, 1987, you may also deduct interest paid on up to $100,000 of home equity debt. Home equity debt is all debt that is secured by your home other than acquisition indebtedness.

Your home plays an important role in your finances. Buying and financing wisely will enhance your ability to accomplish other financial goals.

## MORTGAGE PAYDOWN QUIZ

Are you a candidate for shortening your mortgage?
Select the answer that best describes your situation.

1.  How long do you expect to own your current home

_____  a.  1-4 years

_____  b.  5-9 years

_____  c.  10-20 years

_____  d.  more than 20 years

2.  What percentage of your monthly gross income (before taxes and withholding) is your present house payment (including taxes and insurance)?  Example:  if your house payment is $850 per month and your gross income is $4,000 per month, the percentage is 21%.

_____  a.  less than 18%

_____  b.  18-22%

_____  c.  23-28%

_____  d.  more than 28%

3.  How many months of emergency reserve funds do you have saved?

_____  a.  0-1

_____  b.  2-3

_____  c.  4-5

_____  d.  6 or more months

4. How much consumer debt do you have? (Such as car loans, credit card balances, etc.)

_____ a. less than $2,000

_____ b. $2,000-$5,000

_____ c. $5,001-$10,000

_____ d. more than $10,000

5. What interest rate are you currently paying on your mortgage?

_____ a. less than 7%

_____ b. 7%-10%

_____ c. 10%-13%

_____ d. more than 13%

6. How many years are remaining to payoff your mortgage using your present payment schedule?

_____ a. 24-30 years

_____ b. 18-23 years

_____ c. 13-17 years

_____ d. less than 13 years

## SCORING

Enter your score for each question and total the results.

|     | A | B | C | D | Your Score |
|-----|---|---|---|---|------------|
| 1.  | 1 | 2 | 3 | 4 | _____ |
| 2.  | 4 | 3 | 2 | 1 | _____ |
| 3.  | 1 | 2 | 3 | 4 | _____ |
| 4.  | 4 | 3 | 2 | 1 | _____ |
| 5.  | 1 | 2 | 3 | 4 | _____ |
| 6.  | 4 | 3 | 2 | 1 | _____ |

*Total score* _____

If your score is:

21-24    Begin a program of paying off your mortgage soon. You have much to gain.

17-20    Seriously consider accelerating your mortgage payments to some extent. Be sure to consider all financial factors before deciding how much to add to the payment each month.

12-16    You may want to add a small amount to each monthly payment, but don't overdo it.

5-11    You have other things to be concerned about besides paying off your mortgage. Pay off your other debts, save for emergencies and then take this quiz again.

*Chapter Twelve*
# Maintaining Communication

W hile you and your partner are actually doing the exercises laid out in this book, you are communicating with each other. For long term financial success that communication must continue; it is essential to making this program work. You need to discuss financial matters comfortably and frequently with your partner. And for most couples, such discussions do not happen naturally. Somehow there is always something better to do than talk about money.

Take the bull by the horns and *make* it happen. This chapter details several techniques that can help keep the lines of communication open. Consider which of these techniques might work best for you.

## Family Meeting

One strategy that works well is a family meeting. Having a time planned and set aside for structured discussions increases the chance the meetings will occur. But setting aside time for the meeting is not enough. You need to do some homework to be certain that the discussions are fruitful.

1. Choose an appropriate meeting time. Select a time when both of you are under the least possible stress. Late evening works well.

2. Set a recurring date. The meetings should coincide with a recognizable peak in your financial cycle. For most people, this is the point in each month when the big bills are due. Often the night before the first payday of the month makes the most sense.

3. Structure the meeting. If you sit down and say "Ok, let's talk about money now" nothing will happen except maybe a fight. You should have an agenda for the meeting. This agenda should be similar for every meeting. Sample agenda items are:

   a.   Reread goals statement
- Are we still happy with these goals?
- Are we making progress in reaching these goals?

   b.   Reality check
- How has our cash flow been?
- Is our level of debt really going down?
- Are our liquid assets increasing?

   c.  Immediate concerns
- Bills to pay
- Next month's cash flow
- What else is new?

   d.  Whatever else needs to be discussed
- Analysis of recent decisions
- Emergencies

4. Be prepared for the meeting. The partner responsible for recordkeeping should prepare the documents for the meeting. At the very least a preliminary list of bills to pay needs to be prepared.

These few things will help make your family meeting a powerful tool for good communication.

## WHO'S IN CHARGE?

Most couples find it difficult to divide financial management responsibilities up equitably and efficiently. It's important to identify the tasks that need to be accomplished and then to make sure someone is minding the store. For example, how do you allocate these tasks?

|  | His | Hers |
|---|---|---|
| Paying regular monthly bills | _____ | _____ |
| Balancing checkbooks | _____ | _____ |
| Keeping tax records | _____ | _____ |
| Buying necessities | _____ | _____ |
| Making big purchases | _____ | _____ |
| Preparing net worth statements | _____ | _____ |

Consider assigning most tasks to just one person to create a chief financial officer (CFO) for the family. It is probably more efficient for one person to do all the major record keeping tasks, although we know of couples who successfully sit down to pay the bills together. Be sure that trade-offs are made on other family duties so that the "CFO" position is not too burdensome.

## FEEDBACK

Give yourselves feedback. At some point in the process of making your money work for you, you may have trouble getting a sense of how much you have accomplished. One good check on your progress is to look at your credit card bills to see how much credit card interest you have incurred so far. Most people cut their interest bill in half the first year they actively manage their finances.

Remember, you are not in competition with anyone except your former selves. If you are doing things better in any way than you were before, you are doing great. But, you will not know you have improved unless you recognize achievements and congratulate yourselves for them.

## A Retreat

Some couples find it difficult to schedule un-interrupted time together to discuss goals. One excellent way to get this done is to take a "retreat" together where money is the focus. Plan a week-end at a semi-secluded location where you mutu-ally agree in *advance* to talk about money. It is not fair to surprise your partner with finance when he or she thought romance was the objective of the weekend. Take your most recent net worth state-ment and whatever else you need to set goals including this book. Be specific about when you plan to have your discussion, for example, Satur-day afternoon on the lanai. And do not be sur-prised if it turns out to be romantic too.

A retreat as an annual event can be a powerful tool for keeping a financial plan on track.

## The Non-Stop

The writing technique that you used to set goals can also be helpful in fostering communica-tion. The basic format is to pose an open ended question, each of you write furiously for 10 min-utes, then trade papers to discuss. Remember, to be an effective tool that reveals your partner's inner-most thoughts, non-judgmental discussion is essential.

Here are some topics that lend themselves beautifully to this technique.

- Describe your dream house.
- Describe your ideal vacation.

Create your own questions to spark a lively communication.

*Chapter Thirteen*
# Maintaining Commitment

M aking your money work for you takes staying power. It's great that you have set goals and outlined a savings program. Yet on a day to day basis you need to act to achieve with your goals. Here is where your commitment to your goals becomes essential.

Maintaining commitment over the long run depends upon a variety of factors. In this chapter are a few techniques that have helped others keep committed to their financial success.

### WHAT MESSAGES DO YOU GIVE YOURSELVES?

Many couples point to things outside themselves when they fail to meet their own expectations. They say it was bad breaks or bad advice or bad timing. In some circumstances this may be valid but, more often than not, they are only making excuses for themselves.

If you are committed to achieving financial success or any other kind of success in your lives, be willing to consider what things inside yourselves help or hinder your forward progress.

In particular, consider the concept of self-talk.

Self-talk is based upon the theory that what you believe about yourself (your self-image) has a powerful effect on what you ultimately achieve. Proponents of self-talk suggest that by understanding this concept, and by making positive statements about yourselves, you can increase your successes.

Self-talk helps to create your self-image. It operates as a cycle. Self-talk messages create and reinforce the self-image. A positive self-image leads to actions. Actions support the self-talk. And so it goes.

The power of your beliefs about yourselves is dramatically evident in personal finance. One common self-talk message is, "We cannot save money." This attitude can be destructive to your financial future. Let's look at how it works.

Assume that a couple makes a commitment to saving money for retirement. However, their self-talk conflicts with the goal. The results are unfortunate. They tell themselves that they "cannot save money." Never have, never will. They have created an image of themselves as people who cannot save. So what happens when they are faced with choices? They make the choice consistent with their self-image: they do not save.

Usually, there is not one big choice but a series of small choices, all made in concert with the negative self-image, yielding an unhappy result.

Let's consider a more subtle form of this problem. Probably this couple is trying to overcome their view of themselves as people who do not save. They replace, *"We cannot save money,"* with, *"We will not spend money."* Will that help them turn their plan into action? No. It's still a negative statement. Successful self-talk is both positive and in the present.

Self-talk that is *both* positive and in the present turns the self-image around. For our couple to succeed, they must turn the self-talk to, "We save money."

### Characteristics of Effective Self-Talk

- **Positive** - uses words that talk about doing as opposed to not doing.
- **Present** - uses words that state the image in current terms as opposed to future terms.
- **Specific** - uses words that precisely describe the desired image.

| | | |
|---|---|---|
| Bad | = | We cannot save money. |
| Better | = | We save money. |
| Better yet | = | We save money regularly. |
| Best | = | We save $400 monthly; our bank balance is growing. |

Using self-talk is important to achieving your goals. When you formulate goals, you look to the future. But looking to the future alone will not change your self-talk or your self-image. That change happens in the here and now. Harness the power of self-talk to help you achieve future goals.

## TIMELINE

Do this exercise separately and then compare results.

Draw a line on a piece of paper. Have one end of the line be Today and the other end of the line be your Life Expectancy. Indicate the years along the line.

Today  1 yr  2 yr          Life Expectancy

Plot on your line events that are important to you at the time you expect them to occur. For example you might want to include:

> Birth of children
>
> Children leaving home
>
> Retirement
>
> Parent's life expectancies
>
> Complete education

What does this tell you about your priorities? Does considering your future from this perspective help you become more focused on your goals?

## REWARD YOURSELVES

Keeping your finances on track requires self-discipline on the part of both partners. If you are not naturally highly-organized, motivated types, you may need to build some rewards into your system to keep you going. Even if you are, rewards help to keep up your interest level in your financial strategies.

One place to look for reinforcement is your short-term goals. You may be able to use one of them as a motivation. Hopefully, not all of your goals are serious. Pick one of your more light-hearted short-term goals and agree to achieve that goal a little sooner if you stay on track for a fixed period of time.

A "splurge" can be used as a reward. You might agree to have a splurge at the end of some period of strict adherence to your cash management plan. Weekends out-of-town are a great splurge. Or buying something frivolous you both have been wanting.

However, the real reward is seeing your goals become reality. When looking at your financial information, focus on what has been accomplished. Are you $1,000 less in debt than you were two months ago? Feel good about it. Were you able to write a check to buy your VCR? Feel good about it. Did you say "no" to something you wanted to buy that did not fit in with your goals? That is an achievement. Feel good about it.

## WHATEVER WORKS

There are as many ways of keeping committed to long range goals as there are couples out there who are actually achieving them. Don't hesitate to use any viable technique that fits for you. Remember the object is to have your money start working for you as it never has before. Exactly how you maintain your commitment to the process is not important, the fact that you have maintained commitment is what matters.

*Chapter Fourteen*
# Tool Kit for Success

By this time, you may be overwhelmed with all that you need to do to make your financial goals a reality. Remember, all big jobs boil down to a series of small tasks. Financial success can be reduced to the sum of your day-to-day decisions about earning and spending. Those decisions will be the measure of your ability to capture and put to work some of the cash that comes your way.

This chapter is your tool kit. Included here are several techniques to help you break the larger task of cash management down into manageable pieces.

## PERSONAL ALLOWANCE RULES

An allowance system can help keep your lifestyle costs in line. With such a system, each partner receives a regular allowance to manage his or her personal spending. This provides each of you with privacy and flexibility in spending while keeping the amount in control. You will have to vigorously follow a few simple rules to make allowances really work. Here they are:

1. **The allowance must be taken.** Choose a specified time each week or month for the payment of allowances. It works best within your regular bill-paying cycle. Write the allowance checks on schedule every time. Each partner must take his or her allowance whether needed or not. The checks are smaller only if circumstances change or a permanent reduction is agreed upon. If it is a tough month, both partners take a smaller allowance check.

2. **What is to be paid out of the allowance is agreed upon in advance.** It is not fair to surprise your partner with, "That's supposed to come out of your allowance." Items typically paid out of an allowance are:

- personal care (haircuts, cosmetics, shoe shine),
- commuting (bus fare, parking),
- habits (cigarettes, gum, sodas),
- miscellaneous reading material (*magazines, books, newspapers*)
- gifts (seasonal increase may be required), and
- whatever else works (daily lunches).

3. **Once the allowance is spent, no more until the next allowance.** An allowance is just that. What you get is what you get—and there is not any more where that came from. Obviously, a partner may need an advance on his or her allowance under special circumstances. Consistently running out of money may indicate the allowance is too low. The general rule is the allowance is fixed in amount and timing, and no more money is available.

4. **Never ask your partner what happened to the money.** The whole point is to provide each of you with some *privacy*. How else are birthday and holiday presents to be purchased?

The allowance system gives you the opportunity to be frivolous in a controlled environment. Frivolity is available because you do not have to explain what, when, or why. Frivolity is controlled by the fact that you at some point will run out of money to support it.

And, frankly, not discussing allowances can greatly reduce your opportunities to disagree. Many couples never fight about big money matters, just the little things. Why not avoid it all together? Does it really matter that your partner buys and reads every trashy novel that comes down the pike? Is it worth fighting about? Probably not.

5. **No cheating.** This rule is not as obvious as it seems. The most common (and unconscious) way to cheat is the grocery store gambit. Today, when your friendly neighborhood store sells everything from video games to auto parts, it is easy to cheat. The partner who regularly buys the groceries must be vigilant. Perhaps, you have agreed that miscellaneous reading material must come out of allowances, yet somehow a magazine or two keeps appearing in the grocery cart. Not fair. The correct way to handle it is to separate the items in the cart, write a check for the joint items and pay cash for allowance items.

## BUDGETS

Do not establish a budget for specific living expenses unless your spending behavior is out of control. The purpose of managing your cash is to help you to achieve your goals. As long as your normal living expenses fall consistently within the overall monthly amount that you determined, you will be taking the steps required to achieve those goals. The tedium of monitoring a detailed budget will provide no further benefit.

If you consistently cannot live within your monthly allocation for living expenses, further analysis is probably a good idea. (But this is not the same as budgeting.) In that situation, keep a financial diary with categories of expenses recording everything you spend. Use it to monitor what is happening *daily*. You can only change behavior if you have immediate feedback as to your actions. Totaling everything up at the end of the month is too late. Usually, a short period of daily monitoring is all that is required to turn the problem around.

## BAIT AND SWITCH

One way of taking action to change your behavior is a technique called bait and switch. Many couples find they want to trim the expense of such discretionary items as travel, entertainment, and dining out. Obviously, the expense is cut if you do not travel or dine out. But that reduces the quality of your life rather than enhancing it. A better approach is to figure out what you really like to do, then do it cheaper. The goal is to have the same amount of enjoyment on fewer dollars. Here are some examples of strategies that have worked for others.

**Cheaper restaurants** — Find ethnic or less formal restaurants that serve foods you enjoy. Set a per person dollar limit.

**Drink at home** — Not only will this keep you off the streets if you are inebriated, but also it can reduce your dinner tab substantially.

**Movies at odd hours** — Know the policy of local theaters regarding bargain movie times. You can even see new releases for half price at odd hours. And besides, you are less likely to sit next to a talker in an uncrowded theater.

**Travel off-season** — Reading the travel page in the newspaper can uncover great bargains. Cruising is cheaper in the fall. Sunny destinations are cheaper in the summer. Some ski resorts offer great summertime recreation packages. If you plan to do the unexpected you can often stretch your travel dollar.

**Travel spontaneously** — If you can travel on short notice, tours and cruises can often fit you in for a significant cost reduction.

**Coupons** — Do not be a compulsive coupon clipper, but do use them for products you would buy anyway.

**Stay home** — Consider all the pastimes you may enjoy at home but seldom indulge in. How long has it been since you played Monopoly? How about having friends over for a Fred and Ginger movie festival (potluck, of course)? The possibilities are endless.

**Bulk foods** — Buy in bulk, then use resealable containers to keep what you need fresh. But buy only what you need.

**Wholesalers** — Buy large quantities of staple items at wholesale prices then store them for use.

If you have access to a store that sells wholesale to the public (e.g. Costco, Price Savers, etc.) use it, but stick to staple food and non-food items like paper towels, toilet paper, cat litter, laundry detergent. Buying at wholesale and storing has been estimated to save a family of four as much as $100 to $150 per month. (Large containers of miniature Snickers bars are not staple items for most households.)

**Stop smoking** — No explanation needed.

**Eat less meat** — Recent studies show Americans eat far too much protein anyway. You can reduce portion size rather than serving meatless meals or substitute complex carbohydrates instead.

**Brown bag it** — On days when you are not power lunching consider taking something from home for lunch.

**Cars** — Keep them. Maintain them. Tell them you expect them to last 100,000 miles. If you think you "need" a new car, have old Betsy detailed, then think again.

**Do free (or cheap) stuff** — Keep an eye out for lectures, concerts, or exhibitions at low or no cost.

**Car Rentals** — Rent from a local or smaller agency rather than the national agency right next to baggage claim.

**Flight Insurance** — Do not buy it. You already have enough life insurance, remember?

**Shop carefully for expensive items** — It is worth the time and trouble to shop around for big ticket items like electronics and furniture. Price differences can be enormous.

**Phones** — Buy them. They often pay for themselves in less than one year.

**Clothing** — For any family member who is fully grown, buy good quality that will last, especially leather goods. Take good care of it. For children, try to set a dollar limit and stick to it without sacrificing sturdiness.

**Entertaining at home** — Prepare a per person budget in advance. Try not to prepare too much food (a common mistake). Consider potluck or making assignments of food to bring. Do not assume a caterer is too expensive. Often you can get the food prepared by a caterer and serve it yourself at a reasonable cost.

**Dining out** — Order things you would never make at home (Paella, Steak Diane, Moo Shoo Pork).

**Wine** — If you are serious about wine, a cellar can be a cost saver. Buy cases of young wines and enjoy them when the costs go up.

**Small percentage cost cuts** — Do not punish yourselves. Realistically, you will be most successful at reducing spending if you make small percentage cuts on big items. Food is a good example. Do not expect a family accustomed to spending $500 per month on food to be happy with $300 per month spent on food. It is possible to do, but you may have a riot on your hands! Instead, strive for a five to 10 percent reduction. You will have achieved a lot and no one will notice.

Whatever you do, do not set yourself up to tackle the impossible. If you have high visibility jobs, a one year moratorium on clothes is not realistic. Doing without vacations is probably suicidal. And shorting yourselves on necessary health care or home maintenance may cost you much more money in the future. Make reasonable choices about changing your behavior.

## Cash is King

The secret to successful cash management is strict adherence to the rules. Set income aside, and only take out the agreed upon amount for living expenses **no matter what**.

*Chapter Fifteen*
# Making it Work

Frankly, this approach to making your money work for you is not easy for everyone. It works best when both partners are already willing to communicate with each other and to commit to a goal. If it does not work well for you, do not lose heart. The following are some suggestions that may help you find what *will* work.

### 1. Are you really communicating?

Communication needs to be a continual process. Are both of you honestly expressing your feelings? Are you making yourselves take time to communicate?

Make a date to communicate if need be, but be sure you do it.

### 2. Are both of you committed?

This program will not work in a vacuum. If either of you is not committed, devote an evening to talking about why. Sometimes it means your goals do not adequately reflect both partners' interests and objectives. Consider redoing the goal-setting procedure if this seems to be the case. It is imperative the committed partner not steamroll any goals into the agreed upon goals statement. The goals must be meaningful for both of you.

### 3. Are you capturing your cash?

Actually managing your cash flow and channeling your cash in the directions that you desire is the best evidence that you are making your money work for you. To do this effectively be sure you follow the cash management program to the letter. Pay particular attention to making sure that all income is deposited to the collection account. And watch that only the desired amount for living expenses is being transferred into your checking account(s).

## 4. Have you done everything?

You may have tried to use only the cash management ideas in this book. Perhaps you skipped setting your goals or analyzing your net worth in detail. This program will not work well when you skip steps. Every part of the process—communication, commitment and cash—is essential. If the program is not working for you and you have left something out, start over and *do it all.*

## 5. Do you need extra help?

Perhaps your financial situation is more complex than the situations addressed in the context of this book. Or maybe you need some one-on-one attention to get certain parts of the cash management process completed. Consider working with a Certified Public Account or a Certified Financial Planner to get you on the right track.

The rewards of using **communication, commitment,** and **cash** control are great. You really *can* stop fighting about money and start making your money work for you.

# How to Order
# Work-Size Forms

The trouble with producing a book of this dimension is that the reduced size of the forms and exercises we must use throughout the book make it difficult to actually fill them out.

In order to solve that problem, we've put together a package of all the worksheets and forms used in this book in a convenient 8 1/2" x 11" format.

Just send $3.00 plus .75 shipping & handling, along with your name and address, to: Commonwealth Institute, P.O. Box 8024, Spokane, WA 99203.

We'll send your forms right away, so that you can start making your money work for you even better!